# OLD CHURCH LORE.

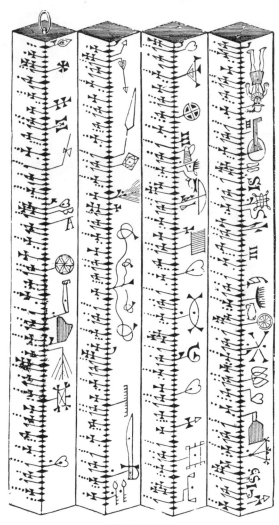

CLOG ALMANACK.

# Old Church Lore.

BY

WILLIAM ANDREWS, F.R.H.S.,

EP Publishing Limited
1975

Republished 1975 by EP Publishing Limited
East Ardsley, Wakefield
West Yorkshire, England


First published 1891 by William Andrews & Co., The Hull Press
Copyright © 1975 EP Publishing Limited


ISBN 0 7158 1137 1

Please address all enquiries to
EP Publishing Limited (address as above)

Printed in Great Britain by
The Scolar Press Limited
Ilkley, West Yorkshire

## Preface.

THE welcome reception from the public and the press accorded to my volume entitled "Curiosities of the Church," has induced me to issue another work on similar lines. Like that book, this one shows how closely the Church in bygone times was linked with the national and social life of the people.

An attempt has been made to blend instruction and entertainment, and present out-of-the-way facts drawn from unpublished documents and other sources, which do not usually come under the notice of the reader.

WILLIAM ANDREWS.

HULL LITERARY CLUB,
*August 1st, 1891.*

# Contents.

|  | PAGE |
|---|---|
| THE RIGHT OF SANCTUARY | 1 |
| THE ROMANCE OF TRIAL | 22 |
| A FIGHT BETWEEN THE MAYOR OF HULL AND THE ARCHBISHOP OF YORK | 37 |
| CHAPELS ON BRIDGES | 44 |
| CHARTER HORNS | 65 |
| THE OLD ENGLISH SUNDAY | 81 |
| THE EASTER SEPULCHRE | 111 |
| ST. PAUL'S CROSS | 120 |
| CHEAPSIDE CROSS | 138 |
| THE BIDDENDEN MAIDS CHARITY | 148 |
| PLAGUES AND PESTILENCES | 152 |
| A KING CURING AN ABBOT OF INDIGESTION | 174 |
| THE SERVICES AND CUSTOMS OF ROYAL OAK DAY | 177 |
| MARRYING IN A WHITE SHEET | 186 |
| MARRYING UNDER THE GALLOWS | 191 |
| KISSING THE BRIDE | 195 |
| HOT ALE AT WEDDINGS | 199 |
| MARRYING CHILDREN | 203 |
| THE PASSING BELL | 210 |
| CONCERNING COFFINS | 218 |
| THE CURFEW BELL | 227 |
| CURIOUS SYMBOLS OF THE SAINTS | 240 |
| ACROBATS ON STEEPLES | 244 |
| INDEX | 253 |

# OLD CHURCH LORE.

## The Right of Sanctuary.

PLACE where criminals and political offenders could find refuge was called a Sanctuary. It is generally agreed that in this country the privilege of sanctuary was instituted on the recognition of Christianity. From an early time down to the days of Henry VIII., fugitives were safe for certain periods in all the churches and churchyards of the land.

The origin of the usage is extremely remote. Most probably it existed among the Israelites before Moses gave directions for the establishment of cities of refuge, when the children of Israel settled in the Promised Land. The Greeks, Romans, Arabs, and American Indians had their places of refuge.

B

In England the laws respecting this subject are both numerous and curious. A code of laws made in the year 693 by Ina, King of the West Saxons, contains a recognition of the right of sanctuary. It is therein stated that, if any one accused of a capital offence takes refuge in a church, his life shall be spared, but the criminal is directed to make compensation for his crime. If the guilty one deserved stripes, they were not to be inflicted. According to Alfred the Great's laws of the year 887, those guilty of slight offences were allowed to flee to a church, and there remain for three nights. Thus time was given them to compound for their misdemeanours, or to make suitable provision for their safety. Stringent measures were taken to guard against the violation of the sanctuary. The person who violated the sanctuary and inflicted bonds, blows, or wounds upon the refugee, had to pay the price set upon his life, and to the officiating ministers of the church, one hundred and twenty shillings, which was a large sum in those days. "If a criminal," says the Rev. J. R. Boyle, f.s.a., in a carefully prepared paper on this theme, "fled to a church, no one should drag him thence within the space of seven days, if he could live so long

without food, and had not attempted to force his
way out. If the clergy had occasion to hold
service in the church whilst the refugee was there,
they might keep him in some house which had no
more doors than the church had."

The law of sanctuary was clearly defined in the
year 1070 by William the Conqueror. The privilege of sanctuary was only temporary, and during
the time of sanctuary, which was within forty
days, the refugee might, if able, come to an
agreement with his adversaries. If he failed to
compound for his crime, he had to appear before
the coroner, clothed in sackcloth, confess his
crime, and abjure the realm. In an act passed in
the year 1529, in the reign of Henry VIII., it is
directed that "immediately after his confession,
and before his abjuration, he was to be branded
by the coroner with a hot iron upon the brawn of
the thumb of his right hand with the sign of the
letter A, to the intent he might be the better
known among the king's subjects to have
abjured." If the offender failed to make a
confession of his crime to the coroner within
forty days, and remained in the sanctuary, any
one found furnishing him with food was regarded
as guilty of felony.

Sir William Rastall, who was Chief-Justice of the Court of Common Pleas, in his "Collection of Statutes now in force," London, 1594, supplies a copy of the form of confession and abjuration usually employed. It is as follows:—

"This hear thou, Sir Coroner, that I............ ............ of............ ............am a............ ............, and because I have done such evils in this land, I do abjure the land of our lord the King, and shall haste me towards the port of [mentioning a port named by the coroner], and that I shall not go out of the highway, and if I do, I will that I be taken as a robber and a felon of our lord the King, and that at such place I will diligently seek for passage, and that I will tarry there but one flood and ebb, if I can have passage; and unless I can have it in such a place, I will go every day into the seas up to my knees assaying to pass over, and unless I can do this within forty days, I will put myself again into the church as a robber and a felon of our lord the King, so God me help and His holy judgment."

The constables of the parishes through which the culprit passed conducted him over their highways to the port from whence he had to embark.

We gather from "England in the Fifteenth Century," by the Rev. W. Denton, M.A., that sanctuary men sent from London to Dover "frequently broke their promise to cross the Channel, betook themselves to the forest, and joined the bands of thieves who made the greenwood of the Weald of Kent their home."

In the reign of Henry VIII. several acts were passed dealing with this subject. The reason why one of the acts was passed was the loss of the strength of the country by persons taking sanctuary and abjuring the realm, teaching foreigners archery, and also of disclosing the secrets of the realm. To prevent such loss, "it was enacted that every person abjuring was to repair to some sanctuary within the realm, which himself should choose, and there remain during his natural life; and to be sworn before the coroner upon his abjuration so to do." If a sanctuary man left his retreat without being granted his discharge by the King's pardon, he ran the risk of being tried for his original crime, and was prohibited from the protective power of the sanctuary. It was usual, in bygone times, for men to wear swords, but when any one took sanctuary he had to give up his weapons, and only use a knife at meal times to cut his meat. The governors of the sanctuaries directed the men under protection to wear a badge or cognisance "openly upon their upper garment, of the compass, in length and breadth, of ten inches," under pain of forfeiting all the privileges of sanctuary. If they left their lodgings between sunset and sunrise it was at the peril of losing all right of protection. In the same reign, it was decreed that persons guilty of high treason, and pirates, should be excluded from the right of sanctuary. The most important measure bearing on this subject, passed in 1540, clearly indicates the adverse attitude assumed by Henry VIII. towards the privilege of sanctuary. He took away the rights from all places except parish churches and their churchyards, cathedrals, hospitals, and the sanctuaries at Wells, Westminster, Manchester, Northampton, Norwich, York, Derby, and Launceston. A year later, Chester was substituted for Manchester. It is stated that the inhabitants of Manchester were much troubled by the influx of dissolute persons seeking sanctuary. They intimated to Parliament that the refugees injured their trade, and further, that as they had "no mayor, sheriff, or bailiff, no walls, and no gaol for the confinement of offenders," they prayed to have the privilege withdrawn. In the statute of 1540, the privilege of sanctuary was "abolished in cases of wilful murder, rape, burglary, highway robbery, or wilful burning of a house or barn containing corn." Not more than twenty persons were to be sheltered in a sanctuary at one time.

An act passed in 1624, in the reign of James I., nominally abolished all privileges of sanctuary in England. It did not completely close all sanctuaries, for in them remained lawless characters, who had long been there, and whom it would not be deemed prudent to have at large. It is asserted that the sanctuary regulations were frequently broken, and that refugees committed robberies and other crimes in the immediate neighbourhood of their sanctuaries.

In the case of debtors, sanctuaries in a modified form existed down to the reign of William III., when, in the year 1697, an Act of Parliament abolished them.

English history furnishes many instances of sanctuary laws being disregarded. A familiar example is that of four Lancastrian knights flying from the battlefield of Tewkesbury, in 1471, and taking refuge in a church not far distant from

the place. Edward, sword in hand, was
about to follow them, and violate the sanctuary,
but the priest who was celebrating mass refused
to permit him to enter, until he agreed to pardon
the knights. He made the promise, whereupon
the refugees left the church. Subsequently they
were made prisoners and executed.

The first time the sanctuary of Westminster
Abbey was violated was in the year 1378. It was
not only violated, but murder was committed.
The particulars of the case are as follow. In one
of the campaigns of the Black Prince, two esquires,
named Frank de Hawle and John Shakle, made
captive a French or Spanish Count. The
prisoner had a friend in John of Gaunt, and he
directed the captors to give up their prize, but
they refused. John of Gaunt, without delay,
imprisoned in the Tower the two men who had
disobeyed his injunctions. They made their
escape, and fled to Westminster Abbey, but were
closely pursued by Sir Allan Boxhull, Constable
of the Tower, Sir Ralph de Ferrers, and a
band of fifty men in arms. It is believed that the
two esquires made their way into the choir of the
Abbey, and at a time when high mass was being
celebrated. " The Deacon," says Dean Stanley,

" had just reached the words of the Gospel of the day, ' If the goodman of the house had known what time the thief would appear——,' when the clash of arms was heard, and the pursuers, regardless of time or place, burst upon the service. Shakle escaped, but Hawle was intercepted. Twice he fled round the choir, with his enemies hacking at him as he ran; and, pierced with twelve wounds, he sank dead in front of the Prior's Stall —that is, at the north side of the entrance of the choir." It is also recorded that his servant and a monk fell at the same time. Hawle was looked upon as a martyr to the injured rights of the Abbey. His remains were laid to rest within its walls, a most unusual honour at that period. The spot where he fell was marked with an inscription engraved on a stone, and over his grave was a brass effigy and a long epitaph, which remained till within the last century. The desecrated Abbey was closed for four months, and the Members of Parliament suspended their sittings within its precincts for fear of pollution. The two chief assailants were excommunicated.

In 1232, the sanctuary of the church at Brentwood, Essex, was violated by orders of the boy king, Henry III. He had allowed himself to be persuaded that the brave Hubert de Burgh had sold his country for French gold, and armed men were sent to make the stout knight prisoner. Hubert took refuge in Brentwood Church. His enemies broke in, dragged him from the very altar, and a smith was ordered to shackle him. " I will die any death," said the smith, " before I put iron on the man who freed England from the stranger, and saved Dover from France ! " so Hubert's feet were tied below his horse, and he was carried to the King. A remonstrance from the Bishop of London caused the refugee to be replaced in the sanctuary, but his foes were still determined to have him. The Sheriff put stakes round the churchyard watched day and night, until hunger compelled a surrender, when Hubert was thrown into prison, and there died.

Elizabeth Woodville, Queen of Edward IV., twice found shelter in the sanctuary of Westminster. Here was born, on April 9th, 1470, Edward V. Skelton, our earliest Poet-Laureate, remained in this stronghold, in safety, writing furious invectives against Cardinal Wolsey. If he had not had the protection of sanctuary, it is believed he would have been doomed to destruc-

tion. " It was impregnable," says Dean Stanley,
"even by all the power of the Cardinal at the
height of his grandeur."

A curious example of the violation of a sanctuary
occurred at Stafford. In the year 1300, a com-
plaint was laid before the King by the Dean and
Chapter of St. Mary's, Stafford, to the effect
that two men imprisoned for felony in Stafford
gaol had escaped, and taken refuge in the church.

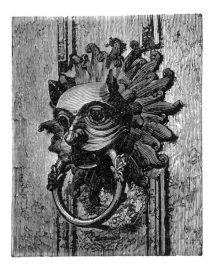

The men were
followed into the
church, captured,
and re-imprison-
ed. The prison
authorities were
directed to restore
the men to the
Dean and Chap-
ter.

It may not be
without interest to
give some details

ANCIENT KNOCKER, DURHAM CATHEDRAL.

of two important north country sanctuaries,
Durham and Beverley. On the north door
of the Cathedral of Durham is a ponderous
bronze knocker, of which we give a drawing.

It will be noticed that the knocker is in the
form of a ring held between the teeth of a
monster's head.   The person claiming sanctuary
raised the ring of the knocker, and sounded it to
obtain admission to the church, where, for a time,
he felt safe out of the reach of his avengers.   In
the sacred building two men were on duty night
and day, ever ready to quickly open the door.   A
bell was next tolled to make known the fact that
a man had taken sanctuary.   When a refugee
sought protection an early intimation was made
to the prior, who gave injunctions that he was
to keep within the limits of the churchyard, which
formed the bounds of the Durham sanctuary.   In
presence of a witness, a detailed account had to
be given of the crime committed, dates, names of
persons, places, etc., had to be given, and they
were carefully noted.   In cases of murder and
manslaughter, the weapon employed had to be
mentioned.   A gown of black cloth, having on its
left shoulder a cross, known as " the cross of St.
Cuthbert," was given him to wear.   The badge
was, we are told, " to the intent that every one
might see that there was such a freelige granted
by God unto St. Cuthbert's shrine, for every such
offender to flee for succour and safeguard of their

lives." The refugee at Durham was allowed the right of sanctuary for thirty-seven days, and provided with food and drink and bedding at the expense of the convent. If within that time he failed to make peace with his adversaries, he had to abjure the realm. He lost his property by this proceeding, but saved his life, or evaded some barbarous form of punishment which often resulted in mutilation of a most painful character.

The Surtees Society, on the 7th December, 1836, resolved to print the Records of the Sanctuaries of Durham and Beverley, and shortly afterwards the work was issued. The Durham notices are reproduced from the ordinary Registers of the Cathedral, and extends from 1464 to 1524. The following shows the number of crimes, and the calling of the men taking refuge :—

Murder and Homicide.—Crimes, 195. Persons implicated, 283. Trades of fugitives :—Husbandmen, 8 ; Labourers, 4 ; Yeomen, 4 ; Gentlemen, 4 ; Ecclesiastics, 3 ; Merchants, 2 ; Tailor, 1 ; Plumber, 1 ; Carpenter, 1 ; Tanner, 1 ; Baxster, 1 ; Glover, 1 ; Sailor, 1 ; Apprentice, 1 ; Under-Bailiff, 1 ; Servant, 1 ; Knight, 1 (an accessory). The occupations of the remainder are not mentioned. Debt, 16. Of these—Shermane, 1 ; Horslibber, 1 ;

Merchant, 1 ; Flesher, 1. Horse-stealing, 4. Of
these—Yeoman, 1. Cattle-stealing, 9. Escaping
from Prison, 4. Of these—Shoemaker, 1. House-
breaking, 4. Rape, 1. Theft, 7. Of these—
Yeoman, 1 ; Ecclesiastic, 1 ; Goldsmith, 1. Back-
ward in his accounts, 1. For harbouring a thief, 1.
For failing to prosecute, 1.

The list of weapons, etc., employed by the
murderers is as under :—

Indefinite, 12 ; Armicudium, 1 ; Arrow, 5 ; Base-
lard 3 ; Bastard-sword, 1 ; Bill, 3 ; Carlisle Axe, 3 ;
Club-staff, 11 ; Crabtree-staff, 1 ; Dagger, 56 ;
Dicker, 1 ; Egelome, 1 ; Forest-bill, 1 ; Halbarde, 2 ;
Hanging, 1 ; Hynger, 3 ; Iron-fork Shaft, 1 ;
Kendal-club, 2 ; Lance, 10 ; Lance-staff, 4 ; Lang
Pike-staff, 1 ; Long Plane-staff, 1 ; Pike-staff, 12 ;
Plane-staff, 1 ; Pychyng-staff, 1 ; Pugio (a dagger),
1 ; Scotch Axe, 2 ; Small-staff, 1 ; Spear-staff, 2 ;
Staff, 14 ; Staff, with a pummel, 1 ; Stone, 2 ;
Sword, 21 ; Trodden to death, 1 ; Turf-spade, 1 ;
Welsh-bill, 6 ; Whynyard (a short dagger), 6 ;
Wood-axe, 3 ; Wood-knife, 1.

The right of sanctuary was granted to the
church of St. John, Beverley, by Athelstan, and
near the altar was placed a Fridstol, or chair of
peace, denoting that here the refugee might find

peace.   According to Camden and Leland, the chair once bore a Latin inscription which has been translated thus : " This stone chair is called the Freed Stool, *i.e.*, the Chair of Peace, to which what criminal soever flies hath full protection." There is not at the present time any trace of an

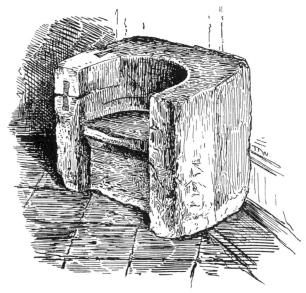

BEVERLEY SANCTUARY CHAIR.

inscription on it.   We only know of two sanctuary chairs which are still preserved in England, namely, one at Beverley and the other at Hexham.

The extent of the Beverley sanctuary was a circle round the church having a radius of about a mile, with the church as a centre,

marked by stone crosses erected on the four
principal roads leading to the town.    " If a malefactor," says Oliver, in his "History of Beverley,"
"flying for refuge was taken or apprehended
within the crosses, the party that took or had hold
of him there, did forfeit two hundreth ; if he
took him within the town, then he forfeited four
hundreth ; if within the walls of the churchyard,
then six hundreth ; if within the church, then
twelve hundreth ; if within the doors of the quire,
then eighteen hundreth, besides penance, as in
case of sacrilege ; but if he presumed to take
him out of the stone chair near the altar, called
Fridstol, or from among the holy relics behind the
altar, the offence was not redeemable with any
sum, but was then become *sine emendatione, boteles*,
and nothing but the utmost severity of the offended
church was to be expected, by a dreadful excom-
munication, besides what secular power would
impose for the presumptuous misdemeanor."
There is a foot-note in Oliver's book, on the
authority of Richard Prior, of Hagulstad, saying
that "the hundreth contained eight pounds ; so
that the last penalty was most immense, nearly as
much as the weregild for killing a crowned head
in Wales ; and, indeed, every act of violence

committed against the right of sanctuary was esteemed a breach of the churches' peace, a high crime, and a species of sacrilege."

The particulars of the persons who took sanctuary from about the year 1478 to 1539, published by the Surtees Society, is drawn from a thin folio volume, preserved among the Harleian MSS. This important manuscript contains a copy of the oath taken by those who sought sanctuary at Beverley. The Bailiff of the Archbishop, by whom the oath was administered, had to enquire of the refugee :—

"What man he killed, and wher with, and both ther names, and than gar him lay his hand uppon the book, saying on this wyse—

Sir, take hede on your oth—Ye shalbe trew and feythfull to my Lord Archbisshop of York, Lord off this towne, to the Provest of the same, to the Chanons of this Chirch, and all other ministers therof.

Also, ye shall bere gude hert to the Baillie and xij governars of this town, to all burges and comyners of the same.

Also, ye shall bere no poynted wepon, dagger, knyfe, ne non other wapen ayenst the Kynge's pece.

Also, ye shalbe redy at all your power, if ther

c

be any debate or stryf, or order so than case of fyre within the towne, to help to surcess it.

Also, ye shalbe redy at the obite of Kyng Adelstan, at the dirige and the messe, at suche tyme as it is done, at the warnyng of the belman of the towne, and doe your dewte in ryngyng, and for to offer at the messe on the morne. So help you God and thies holy Evangelistes. And than gar hym kysse the book."

The Bailiff's fee on this occasion appears to have been two shillings and fourpence, that of the Clerk of the Court, for inscribing the name of the refugee in the register, fourpence.

As we have previously stated, the Beverley register, published by the Surtees Society, commences about the year 1478, and extends to 1539. A summary of the crimes and the trades, etc., of refugees is as follows :—

Crimes.—Indefinite, 35.    Persons concerned, 35.    No trade described, 10; Labourers, 3; Tylers, 2 ; Tailors, 2 ; Masons, 2 ; Dyers, 2 ; Yeomen, 2 ; Merchant, 1 ; Husbandman, 1 ; Smith, 1 ; Clerk, 1 ; Butcher, 1 ; Chapman, 1 ; Gentleman, 1 ; Draper, 1 ; Skinner, 1 ; Shoemaker, 1 ; Haberdasher, 1 ; Litster, 1.    Murder and Homicide.— Crimes, 173.    Persons implicated, 186.    No trade

or occupation described, 52; Tailors, 19; Husband-
men, 17; Yeomen, 16; Labourers, 14; Weavers
and Websters, 11; Shoemakers, 8; Butchers, 6;
Gentlemen, 6; Mercers, 3; Barbers, 3; Brewers, 3;
Servants, 2; Esquires, 2; Surgeons, 2; Millers, 2;
Mariners, 2; Smith, 1; Shearman, 1; Spinster, 1;
Carpenter, 1; Painter, 1; Chapman, 1; Maltster, 1;
Cartwright, 1; Gentlewoman, 1; Chandler, 1;
Minstrell, 1; Cooper, 1; Literate, 1; Saddler, 1;
Shepherd, 1; Carrier, 1; Tanner, 1; Cook, 1;
Hatmaker, 1. Felony.—Crimes, 51. Persons
implicated, 54. No trade described, 3; Labourers,
8; Tailors, 6; Husbandmen, 4; Butchers, 4;
Glovers, 3; Goldsmiths, 3; Cutlers, 3; Tylers, 2;
Plumbers, 2; Yeomen, 2; Merchant, 1; Smith, 1;
Clerk, 1; Physician, 1; Spinster, 1; Grocer, 1;
Gentleman, 1; Pinner, 1; Mariner, 1; Shoemaker,
1; Fishmonger, 1; Fuller, 1; Brickmaker, 1.
Horse stealing, 1, a Labourer. Treason, 1, a
Butcher. Receipt of stolen goods, 1, a Haber-
dasher. Coining.—Cases, 6; persons, 7. No
trade described, 1; Yeomen, 2; Fleshers, 2;
Tailor, 1; Weaver, 1. Debtors, 208. No trade
described, 36; Butchers, 31; Labourers, 12;
Merchants, 9; Husbandmen, 9; Gentlemen, 9;
Mercers, 8; Tailors, 6; Weavers and Websters, 5;

Dyers, 5 ; Yeomen, 5 ; Glovers, 4 ; Drapers, 4 ;
Shearmen, 3 ; Chapmen, 3 ; Pewterers, 3 ; Smiths,
2 ; Grocers, 2 ; Fishers, 2 ; Bakers, 2.; Chandlers, 2 ;
Wheelwrights, 2 ; Coopers, 2 ; Pouchmakers, 2 ;
Vintners, 2 ; Fishmongers, 2 ; Bowyers, 2 ; Tapper,
1 ; Alderman and Grocer of London, 1 ; Carpenter,
1 ; Wax Chandler, 1 ; Painter, 1 ; Goldsmith, 1 ;
Clothier, 1 ; Waiter, 1 ; Maltster, 1 ; Surgeon, 1 ;
Pinner, 1 ; Skinner, 1 ; Fustain Shearer, 1 ;
Capper, 1 ; Mason, 1 ; Haberdasher, 1 ; Salter, 1 ;
Carrier, 1 ; Tanner, 1 ; Woolman, 1 ; Purser, 1 ;
Singingman, 1 ; Woodmonger, 1 ; Cook, 1 ;
Wooldriver, 1 ; Hatmaker, 1 ; Bedmaker, 1 ;
Barber, 1.

The weapons employed in cases of murder are
seldom named in the Beverley records.

The right of sanctuary was, perhaps, a blessing
in the time it existed. Hallam, in his "State of
Europe in the Middle Ages," says that right of
sanctuary might as often be a shield of innocence
as an impunity of crime. "We can hardly regret,
on reflecting on the desolating violence which prevailed, that there should have been some green
spots in the wilderness, where the feeble and the
persecuted could find refuge. How must this
right have enhanced the veneration for religious

institutions! How gladly must the victims of internal warfare have turned their eyes from baronial castle, the dread and scourge of the neighbourhood, to those venerable walls, within which not even the clamour of arms could be heard to disturb the chaunt of holy men and the sacred service of the altar."

## The Romance of Trial.

IN past ages, trial by ordeal was customary in this country, and at the present time in several foreign lands, where education has not swept away superstitious beliefs, it is often used as a means of testing the guilt or innocence of accused persons. The origin of ordeal may be traced back to a remote period. In the Anglo-Saxon judicial systems it formed an important feature, and the first record of it in this country appears in the laws of King Ina, who reigned over Wessex from the year 688 to 727. The clergy figured prominently in the trials.

For three days prior to the time appointed for the trial, the accused passed through a course of severe discipline and austere diet. He declared on oath that he was innocent of the crime laid to his charge. Twenty-four of his friends and foes

were brought together, and after a religious
service, specially prepared for the occasion, had
been performed, the ordeal was then tried. The
ordeals were of various kinds, the nobles and
other great personages being generally tried with
the boiling water ordeal.

A ring or piece of metal, blessed by the priest,
was cast into the boiling water, and on either side
of the vessel were ranged the twelve friends and
the twelve foes to witness the due execution of
justice. The arm of the accused was bared,
he plunged it into the liquid and brought out
the article deposited in it by the priest. The
degree of the crime regulated the depth of the
water; if slight, it only reached to the wrist, but if
serious, the arm was dipped up to the elbow, or
even higher. The priest quickly bound up the
arm, and the bandages were not removed for
three days. At the end of that time, if the priest
pronounced the arm healed, the sufferer was
regarded as guiltless; if not, it was believed that
God had interposed and convicted him.

Deputies sometimes performed the ordeals.
A notable instance of employing a substitute is
that of Theatberge, wife of Lothaire, of France.
She confessed to having been guilty of incest, but

subsequently recanting, it was decided to try her by the ordeal, and a ring was thrown into boiling water according to custom. The Queen elected a proxy, and it is recorded of him whom she chose that he "produced the ring without injuring his hand, in spite of the fire under the caldron being so intense that the water boiled over."

It is asserted that the familiar saying of going "through fire and water" for any one is derived from the practice of employing deputies in the performance of ordeals.

In Mr. James Forbes' "Oriental Memoirs," published 1813-15, are some details of boiling oil ordeals. One of the cases relates to the coolies of a village in the northern part of Guzerat, who were charged with seizing and imprisoning a Bohra, and extorting a bond from him for 450 rupees. The chief denied the charge, and offered to prove his innocence by trial by ordeal. We are told that "a large copper pot full of oil was put on a fire in the market-place, and a pair of black-smith's bellows applied to blow the fire until the oil became very hot." A rupee was thrown into the boiling oil. The chief next declared his innocence, said his prayers, plunged his hand into the boiling liquid, and brought out the coin. He next exhibited his hand to the spectators, when no traces of scalding could be detected; indeed it appeared as if it had been dipped in cold oil. Himself and his tribe were pronounced not guilty of the charge, and he was dismissed with the gift of a turban.

The cold water ordeal appears to have been usually employed to try the humbler classes. The accused went through fasting and discipline similar to the trial by boiling water. After attending church, the person on trial was conducted to a deep pool, and then bound hand and foot with cords. The priest next adjured the water to receive the accused into its bosom if innocent, but to reject him if he were guilty. He was cast into the water. If he sank he was deemed innocent, and was at once drawn out by a rope which had previously been tied round his waist. We gather from Hallam's "Middle Ages" that a citizen of London, having failed in the ordeal of cold water, was hanged by the order of Henry II. The man tried to save his life by offering 500 marks. In cases of murder, if the accused even went through the ordeal of water, he was banished from the realm.

Some attention is paid to this ordeal by Dr. Charles Mackay, in his "Popular Delusions." "It was," he says, "a trial of the poor and humble, and whether they sank or swam was thought of very little consequence. Like witches of more modern times, the accused were thrown into a pond or river. If they sank they were drowned, their friends had the consolation that they were innocent; if they swam they were guilty. In either case society was rid of them." We believe there is little foundation in fact for the foregoing statement by Dr. Mackay. After careful investigation we have not found a record of persons being drowned. The rope fastened to the body of the accused would prevent any such accident.

Towards the close of the twelfth century the use of this ordeal was very general. Lea, in his "Superstition and Force," says that "The assizes of Clarendon, in 1166, confirmed at Northampton in 1176, direct an inquest to be held in each shire, and all who are indicted for murder, robbery, harbouring of malefactors, are to be at once, without further trial, passed through the water ordeal to determine their guilt or innocence." Mr. Lea thinks that the basis of this ordeal may be traced back to the primitive Aryans, who believed that the pure element would not receive into its bosom a person stained with the crime of a false oath.

Many strange stories are related respecting the ordeal of red-hot iron; and not a few of a tragical character. There were two ways of performing the red-hot iron ordeal. One was by taking up a piece of red-hot iron, weighing from one to three pounds, or walking barefoot and blindfolded over nine red-hot ploughshares placed lengthwise at irregular distances. If the accused passed through this ordeal without being hurt he was deemed innocent. There is a popular story that Emma, the mother of Edward the Confessor, was charged with undue familarity with Alwyn, Bishop of Winchester. She proved her innocence by passing unharmed over heated plough-shares.

Among the many instances of persons tried by this ordeal of hot iron may be mentioned Remigius, the Bishop of Dorchester, who was accused of treason against William the Conqueror. One of the bishop's followers underwent the ordeal, and cleared his lordship of the charge.

It has been suggested by some authorities

on this subject that the apparently hot iron was really cold and painted red. In some instances the hands and feet were perhaps rubbed with certain compositions which would enable the persons going through the ordeal to touch the iron without doing injury to themselves. We know that in our own time, to shew the power of resisting fire is not by any means a difficult feat, and it often forms an item on the programmes of popular entertainments.

Shakspeare and other writers refer to the ancient superstition that the wounds of a murdered person would bleed again if touched by the murderer. In *Richard III.*, the dramatist writes as follows respecting Richard, Duke of Gloster :—

> "O gentlemen, see, see! dear Henry's wounds
> Open their congeal'd mouths and bleed afresh!
> Blush, blush, thou lump of foul deformity;
> For 'tis thy presence that exhales this blood
> From cold and empty veins, where no blood dwells;
> Thy deed, inhuman and unnatural,
> Provokes this deluge most unnatural."

Stow, in his "Annals," records that the king's body "was brought to St. Paul's in an open coffin, barefaced, where he bled; thence he was carried to Blackfriars, and there bled."

King James, in his "Dæmonologie," thus refers to this superstition : "In a secret murder," says the King, "if the dead carkasse be at any time thereafter handled by the murderer, it will gush out of blood, as if the blood were crying out to heaven for the revenge of the murderer." Dryden adverts to the theme:—

> "If the vile actors of the heinous deed
>   Near the dead body happily be brought,
>   Oft hath been proved the breathless corpse will bleed."

This ordeal in bygone times was frequently tried, and it was the means of bringing not a few murderers to justice. In some instances the details of the crimes and their detection read more like romance than a statement of facts.

In the olden days witnessing an execution was a sight not to be missed by old or young folk ; even children wended their way to the fatal tree. Sir Symonds D'Ewes, the antiquary, in his boyhood days, attended the execution of a man named Babb, and subsequently wrote an account of the painful circumstances connected with the case. We gather from his notes that Babb had formerly lived near to Wambrook, on the southern border of Somerset. He had sought in vain for the hand in marriage of a widow living

near Taunton. She, however, declined his proposal. Babb, although greatly disappointed at
his failure, resolved to make one more attempt to
win the woman. He hid himself in a brewhouse
used by the widow, and when she appeared he
once more pressed his suit. She heard him with
disdain, and almost before he had finished his
speech she said, " Have thee, base rascal ? No !"
She then struck him on the head with a pewter
candlestick. This made his blood boil, and he
inflicted upon her sixteen wounds, causing her
death. Afterwards, he put the knife in her hand,
making it appear as if she had committed suicide,
and then quietly stole away from the place.

The unfortunate widow was buried, but tongues
and brains were not set at rest, for it was the
opinion of not a few that she had met her death
at the hands of a murderer. Amongst the active
in this matter was a leading local magistrate,
named Mr. Ware, Hestercombe House, near
Taunton. Like other people of this period,
he believed in the ordeal by touch. "This
active magistrate," we find stated, "caused
the body to be disinterred, that all the inhabitants
living within a circle of three miles might
assemble to touch the body, and go through

this powerful ordeal. Babb ran away to escape this dreadful mode of testing the inhabitants' innocence. His racking conscience gave him no repose; he returned and yielded himself up to justice." At the next county assizes for Somerset, held at Chard, in the year 1613, he was tried, found guilty, and condemned to death. Shortly afterwards he was hanged near Wambrook.

Charles I. presented to Dr. Wren, the father of the famous Sir Christopher Wren, the rectory of Great Haseley, near Oxford. During his incumbency, occurred a sad event, which made a great impression on his mind. He detailed, in Latin, particulars of the matter, and duly attested the truth by signing it. Lucy Phillimore, the author of an ably-written work on "Sir Christopher Wren: his Family and his Times," supplies an English version of the tragedy. "Among the retainers of Lord Norris," we are told, "was an old man who had charge of the fish ponds; he had one nephew, who was the heir of all his uncle's possessions and savings. The nephew enticed the old man out one night, waited till he fell asleep under an oak tree, murdered him by a blow on the head, dragged the body to one of the ponds, tied a great stone to the neck, and threw the corpse in. There it lay five weeks, during which time Lord Norris and all the neighbours wondered what had become of the old man. At length, attracted to the spot by the swarms of flies, the body was found by the men who were about to clean the pond. They raised the corpse with great difficulty, and recognised it. The stone tied to the neck was evidence of foul play, though no one could guess the murderer. Lord Norris, in order to detect the criminal, after the usual manner, commanded that the corpse, preserved by the water from the last extremity of decay, should, on the next Sunday, be exposed in the churchyard, close to the church door, so that every one entering the church should see and touch it. The wicked nephew shrank from the ordeal, feigning to be so overwhelmed with grief as to be unable to bear the sight of his dearest uncle. Lord Norris, suspecting that the old man had been murdered by the one person whom his death would profit, compelled him to come, and to touch with his finger, as so many had willingly done, the hand of the dead. At his touch, however, 'as if opened by the finger of God, the eyes of the corpse were seen by all to move, and blood to flow from his nostrils.' At this awful witness, the murderer fell on the ground and avowed the crime, which he had secretly committed, and the most just judgment of God had brought to light." The murderer was tried before one of His Majesty's judges, and the circumstances of the crime fully stated. He was condemned to death, and the sentence was duly carried out by the hangman.

Another strange story comes down to us from the days when the first Charles was king. It relates to Herefordshire. Johan Norkeff was found dead, and it was believed that she had laid violent hands upon herself. After she had been buried about a month, circumstances caused it to be suspected that she had met her death by foul play. The case came under the consideration of a coroner and jury, and they finally resolved to have the body exhumed, and cause the four suspected persons to touch it. The result of the ordeal was narrated at the assizes by an old minister as follows : " The body being taken out of the grave and laid on the grass, the accused were required to touch it. On laying on their hands on the brow, which before was of a livid and carrion colour, it began to have a dew or gentle

D

sweat upon it, which increased by degrees until
the sweat ran down the face. The brow then
turned to a lifelike and flesh colour, and the dead
woman opened one of her eyes and shut it again,
and this opening of the eye was done three times.
She likewise thrust out the ring or marriage
finger three times, and the finger dropped blood
on the grass." The old minister swore to the
correctness of the foregoing, and, says James
Grant, in "The Mysteries of all Nations," from
whom we draw the evidence, another clergyman
corroborated it. Sir Nicholas Hyde, the eminent
lawyer, who rose to be Lord Chief Justice,
questioned the correctness of the evidence, but
the members of the jury did not agree with him,
finding three of the prisoners guilty of murder.
Two were executed, and the third, a woman,
was reprieved.

On much weaker evidence to the preceding
cases, Philip Stanfield was condemned, in 1688,
for the murder of his father, Sir James Stanfield.
An account of the matter will be found in
Chambers's "Domestic Annals of Scotland,"
vol. 2, pages 491-92. The case may be briefly
stated as follows: The body of Sir James
Stanfield, of New Mills, was found in a stream

near Haddington. It appeared that he had met his dead by strangling. James Muirhead, a surgeon, and another person swore that when Philip Stanfield was helping to place the body of his father in a coffin, blood started from the left side of his neck upon his touch, and that he exclaimed, " Lord have mercy upon me ! " On this slight evidence he was, 7th February, 1688, pronounced guilty of parricide, and was publicly executed on the 24th of the same month, and his body hung in chains. He protested his innocence to the last. " The whole case," says Dr. Robert Chambers, "seems to be a lively illustration of the effect of superstitious feeling in blinding justice."

On the 14th June, 1641, a commission which sat at Dalkeith, pronounced Christina Wilson guilty of the death, by sorcery, of her brother, Alexander Wilson. She had been, prior to the trial, directed by the minister and others to touch the corpse of her brother. After an earnest prayer, in which she fervently prayed to God, who had made the sun to shine on their home, to bring the murderer to justice, she touched the body. It bled, although it had not done so when touched by others. This was deemed sufficient proof of her guilt, and on this evidence she suffered death.

With directing the attention to the survival of touching the dead, we must draw to a close our study of the romance of trial. In the north of England, and other parts of the country, it is the practice of persons who come to see a corpse to touch it, as a token "that they wished no ill to the departed, and were at peace and amity with them."

## A Fight between the Mayor of Hull and the Archbishop of York.

THE prelates of the past enjoyed not a few peculiar privileges which are not inherited by their successors in modern times. In the mediæval era, the dignitaries of the church led comparatively exciting lives, and were by no means strangers to the use of sword and lance, many gaining fame on the field of battle.

Representatives of the church often possessed rights in respect to the gallows and its victims. A few facts about a case occurring far back, in the days of our first Edward, shew how keenly they maintained their privileges. The Abbot of Peterborough set up a gallows at Collingham, Nottinghamshire, and had hanged thereon a thief. This proceeding came under the notice of the Bishop of Lincoln, and he, with considerable warmth and temper, declared that the Abbot had usurped his rights, since he held from the king's predecessors the liberty of the Wapentake of Collingham, and the right of executing criminals. The Abbot declared that Henry III. had given to him and his successors " Infangthef and Utfangthef in all his hundreds and demesnes." After investigation it was decided that the Abbot was in the wrong, and he was directed to take down the gallows he had erected. One, and perhaps the chief, reason of the prelate being so particular to retain his privileges was on account of it entitling him to the chattels of the condemned criminals.

William the Conqueror invested the Abbot of Battle Abbey with authority to save the life of any malefactor he might find being executed, and whose life he wished to spare.

Amongst the many privileges enjoyed by the Archbishop of York, was that of having a mint. As early as the year 1070, we find a mention of the mint, and particulars of attempts made, without success, to destroy or curtail His Grace's coining. Archbishop Lee, who died in 1544, is said to have been the last to exercise the power of issuing money.

In bygone times, the Archbishops of York appear to have enjoyed almost regal power. The baronies of Beverley, Sherburn, Patrington, Otley, and Wilton belonged to them. They appointed justices for these important towns, had prisons, gallows, pillories, and ducking stools, and did their utmost to maintain law and order.

It will be gathered from the foregoing that prelates were granted privileges which enabled them to exercise much power amongst the people. Some of the rights enjoyed at Hull by the Archbishop of York were oppressive to the inhabitants of the town, and gave rise to much strife. It was the practice, exercised according to ancient custom, of the Archbishop of York to claim prisage from every vessel of twenty tons burden entering the river Hull. Two casks of wine were demanded, one from before and the other from behind the mast. The casks, however, might be redeemed by paying twenty shillings for each cask. The merchants successfully evaded payment of duty by unloading their ships in the Humber, and bringing their goods into port in small craft. As may be readily expected, the Archbishop was much annoyed at the conduct of the men of Hull, who received the support of the

Mayor of the town ; indeed, if we read history aright, we find the local authorities had a desire to enjoy the privileges claimed by the prelate. A great difficulty had been experienced for a long time by the officers of the Archbishop in collecting the dues, and Archbishop Neville saw that unless he made a firm stand to maintain his privileges, they would be lost. In the year 1378, he decided to visit Hull, and enforce his rights. The Mayor of Hull, at that time was Sir Thomas de Waltham, a knight of quick temper, and with no particular respect for persons with whom he came in contact.

The Archbishop, with a few attendants, numbering less than a dozen, came to the town. The Mayor, accompanied by two bailiffs, named John Arnold and Thomas Green, and a large company of local supporters, met His Grace. The Archbishop complained bitterly to the Mayor, saying, amongst other serious faults, that he had shown himself wanting in that respect for the Archbishop which the representative of religion was entitled to receive. His Worship soon waxed warm, declaring that he had only done his duty in maintaining the rights of his fellow-townsmen. The prelate insisted that the

Mayor was in the wrong, and that it was his
intention to enforce the payment of his dues.
The Mayor soon shewed signs of his displeasure,
and seeing one His Grace's men mocking him,
he, without ceremony, snatched from the Archbishop his crosier, and struck the man. This
was the commencement of a free fight, in which
the prelate and his people suffered a severe
defeat. Blood freely flowed, and the Archbishop,
seeing that he could not make, with any degree
of success, a stand against so many opponents,
beat a hasty retreat, followed a considerable
distance out of the town by a large number of
excited inhabitants of Hull, eager to avenge the
wrongs it was believed His Grace had done to
the port by collecting, or attempting to collect,
prisage. The Mayor, it must be recorded,
fought manfully with the crosier, which was
broken into several pieces.

The Archbishop, being a Court favourite,
brought the matter under the notice of the King.
The Mayor was summoned to appear before His
Majesty at Westminster. This proceeding
doubtless caused much trouble in Hull, but the
Mayor, feeling that he had right on his side,
proceeded to London with a brave heart, and at

the trial pleaded his cause with considerable
eloquence.   The case resulted in judgment being
left in abeyance, or, in other words, His Grace
was non-suited.

We can readily imagine that the Mayor would
return home in higher spirits than when he left it
to appear in the King's Court, and that he would
receive a hearty welcome from his fellow townsmen.

The place where the fight occurred was
regarded by the superstitious as sacred, crowds
of fanatics repairing to it to shed tears.   Not a
little inconvenience was caused by their conduct,
and their proceedings were stopped by a
permanent guard being appointed to keep folk
away from the place.

After the death of the Archbishop, it was
believed for many years that his spirit haunted
the spot where the battle was fought.

In spite of the serious breach between Prelate
and Mayor, Hull appears to have been a
favourite residence in past times of the Archbishops of York.   We know, from the annals of
the town, that in the year 1442 the Archbishop
had a house in the historic High Street.

Dr. Thomson, the late Archbishop of York,

was a frequent and welcome visitor to the town. The last time he was in Hull, His Grace was the guest of Alderman Sherburn, the Mayor. When we saw the two gentlemen in friendly conversation, we could not help contrasting the conditions of 1889 with those of 1378, and noting the great changes which five centuries have brought about, changes better alike for gentle and simple.

## Chapels on Bridges.

THE building of bridges in bygone times was regarded as a religious duty. An order of friars was established on the continent, in the twelfth century, having for its object the erecting and repairing of bridges. Its work extended into several countries. In France, the friars built the celebrated bridge over the Rhone at Avignon, and a bridge, still in use, at Pont St. Esprit, was one of their works. We have not any traces of the operations of the order in England, but there were in the country, prior to the reign of Richard II., lay-brotherhoods performing a similar good work.

Queen Matilda erected and endowed bridges at Stratford and Bow, which she regarded as meritorious. The Church looked upon the work as one deserving of encouragement. Richard

de Kellawe, Bishop of Durham, from 1311 to
1316, for example, promised to remit penances
for those engaged in bridge-building. The
Registry of his Episcopal Chancery contains
many entries similar to the following:
"Memorandum . . . his lordship grants forty
days' indulgence to all who will draw from the
treasure that God has given them, valuable and
charitable aid towards the building and repair of
Botyton bridge." We read in another entry:
"Forty days' indulgence is allowed to those
sincerely contrite and confessed of all their sins,
who shall help by their charitable gifts, or by
their bodily labour, the building and maintenance
of the causeway between Brotherton and Ferry-
bridge, where many people pass by." On
another occasion, a similar indulgence was
granted for help towards the highroad and
bridge between Billingham and Norton.

The most striking case which has come under
our notice, where pious motives have caused the
erection of a bridge, is set forth in a contract of
the thirteenth century. The particulars are
given in Jusserand's "English Wayfaring Life in
the Middle Ages." "Reginald de Rosels," we
are told, "allowed Peter, Abbot of Whitby, to

build a permanent bridge on the river Esk, between his own and the convent's lands. He pledges himself in that act to permit to all comers free access to the bridge through his own property. 'For which concession the aforesaid Abbot and convent have absolved in chapter all the ancestors of the same Reginald of all fault and transgression they may have committed against the church of Whiteby, and have made them participant of all the good works, alms, and prayers of the church of Whiteby.'" The original contract is in Latin, and was printed by the Surtees Society (1881).

"It was very usual," says Leland, "in greater brydges to build chappells in which they did pray for the soules of their founders." There were other reasons for erecting chapels, one being for a place of residence for priests to solicit alms from all who passed over the bridge, whether walking or riding, to keep it in repair. Some were built for sheltering benighted travellers, having crypts where rest and refreshment might be obtained. In these chapels, the wayfarer could pray for protection on his journey, and return thanks for safety after his undertaking had been completed. Travelling, in mediæval times, was beset with trial and hardship on every side.

The history and romance of London Bridge must ever remain amongst the subjects most popular to the people of England. The first and

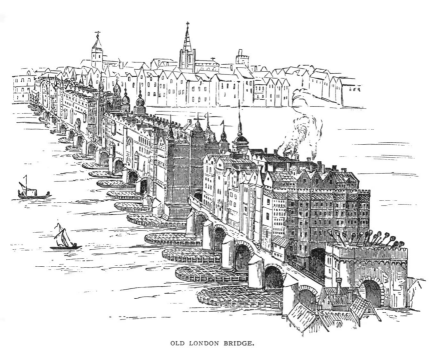

OLD LONDON BRIDGE.

famous London Bridge was regarded as one of the glories of the Middle Ages. The bridge was commenced by Peter Colechurch, in 1176. He worked for twenty-nine years, then death ended his earthly career, and "he was sepultured" in the chapel on the bridge he had done so much to erect. A clever Frenchman, called Isembert, completed the work, in the year 1209. The undertaking had the hearty support of the people, and large sums of money and extensive endowments of land were given to carry it on. The excitement throughout the land was immense. The nation felt it was one of its great undertakings. It was in length nine hundred and twenty-six feet, in width forty feet, some sixty feet above the water, and stood upon nineteen pointed arches, between massive piers. When first completed, it had only one building upon it, a handsome stone chapel, dedicated to St. Thomas Becket, which stood on the middle pier. Subsequently, two rows of houses were erected on the bridge, one on each side of the road. A drawbridge was put up as a means of protection. A terrible fire, on July 10th, 1212, was the cause of the death of upwards of 3,000 persons. Stow, in his " Survey of London," supplies some important information on this subject. After adverting to a fire commencing on the Southwark side of the bridge, he states that " an exceeding great multitude of people passing the bridge, either to extinguish and quench it, or else to gaze at and behold it, suddenly the north part, by blowing of the south wind, was also set on fire, and the people, which were even now passing the bridge, perceiving the same, would have returned, but were stopped by fire ; and it came to pass, that as they stayed or protracted time, the other end of the bridge also, namely, the south end, was fired, so that the people, thronging themselves between the two fires, did nothing else but expect present death ; then came there to aid them many ships and vessels, into the which the multitude so unadvisedly rushed that, the ships being drowned, they all perished. It was said, that through the fire and shipwreck, there were destroyed about three thousand persons, whose bodies were found in part, besides those that were wholly burnt to ashes, and could not be found." A frost, in 1282, destroyed five arches of the bridge. In 1305, when Edward I. was king, was commenced the practice of placing the heads of traitors over London Bridge gateway. Paul Hentzner, a German traveller, visited England in 1598, and counted on it no fewer than thirty heads. Several houses on the bridge were destroyed by fires at various times, and all

E

were swept away by the Great Fire, of 1666. A
good idea of these buildings may be obtained
from the picture we give on page 47.

On the west side of the Ouse Bridge, at York,
was St. William's Chapel, an interesting example
of early English architecture.    Respecting the
origin of this chapel, there is a popular story
that it was built shortly after the bridge was
completed, in 1268, in obedience to royal
commands.    The tale is to the effect that a
Scotch nobleman was visiting the city, shortly
after the erection of the bridge, when some of the
citizens quarrelled and came to blows with his
servants on the bridge.    Several of the strangers
were slain.    The riot was brought under the
notice of the kings of England and Scotland for
settlement, and it was finally agreed that the
citizens of York should pay £300, a large amount
in those days, and erect a chapel on or near the
spot where the servants met their untimely
deaths, and also that they maintain two priests to
pray for the souls of the slain men.    After the
Reformation, the chapel was converted into an
Exchange for the Society of Hamburg
Merchants at York, and subsequently put
to other secular uses.    Finally it was taken

down, on the erection of a new bridge, in the year 1810.

Under the year 1505, a note appears in Hollinworth's "Mancuniensis," stating that "Care was taken for the reparation of the chappell standing on Salford Bridge, built, as it is sayd, by Thomas del Booth, in Edward III.'s time. He certainly gave £30 towards the building of Salford Bridge; and it was very usual on greater bridges to build chappells, in which they did pray for the soules of their founders. This chappell is now converted to a prison for Manchester and Salford." The building was pulled down in 1778, for the purpose of making the bridge wider.

We have other instances of bridge prisons besides the one at Salford. A familiar example is that at Bedford. It has been asserted by several authors that Bunyan was imprisoned in it, but it has been proved beyond doubt that such was not the fact. The bridge prison belonged absolutely to the borough, and Bunyan was a county prisoner, and spent his time in the county gaol. Much interesting information bearing on this subject will be found in Dr. Brown's book on Bunyan. The records of the town contain some

curious particulars respecting the bridge. The
following may be given as an example : " Item,

BRADFORD BRIDGE.

yt ye ordered that the great cheyne by every
nighte at ten of the clocke to be locked crosse the

great bridge, and so kept untyl fyve of the clocke in the morninge, and that he or they that shall dwell in the bridge house, to keep the keye of the said locke, and keep the same soe locked, and not suffer aine horse, horseman, or cattell to passe within that tyme wch he shall not knowe. And of them wch he shall knowe, to take a pennie only for letting doune the cheyne and noe more." The prison was taken down in the year 1765. Here was a chapel or oratory, dedicated to St. Thomas the Martyr, built by a Bedford man, early in the fourteenth century, and endowed with lands for the support of a warden or chaplain, who had to repair the bridge at his own expense.

A small structure on the old bridge at Bradford-on-Avon has also been used as a prison. Its original purpose has provoked some discussion. Some say that it was erected for a chapel, but not a few question the statement. Aubrey of old, and the Rev. J. Charles Cox, LL.D., and Precentor Venables of our time, are of opinion that it was a chapel. For many years it was used as a lock-up, and later as a powder magazine. It has a dome-like roof, of later date than the building. It bears a model of a gudgeon, the emblem of St. Nicholas. The Bradford-on-Avon folk are familiarly spoken of as Bradford gudgeons. Those who had been imprisoned on the bridge were said to have been "under fish and over water."

A small bridge-chapel at Derby, dedicated to St. Mary of the Brigg, links the past with the

ST. MARY'S BRIDGE-CHAPEL, DERBY.

present. It most probably dates back to the fourteenth century. Rev. J. Charles Cox, LL.D., in his "Churches of Derbyshire," traces with care the history of this old-time building. He says: "St. Mary's Bridge—by which access was gained from Nottingham and the south into the town of

Derby, through whose streets lay one of the most important thoroughfares from London to the north—must, in mediæval days, have been of considerable importance. It is pleasant to think of the busy burgesses or men-at-arms turning aside into the Chapel of Our Lady for a brief silent prayer, before crossing the Derwent, and plunging into the forests that stretched out before them on the other side of the river." There would, doubtless, be a gatehouse, built for defence and for levying tolls, etc. On the chapel or gatehouse were placed the heads and quarters of the priests who were martyred at Derby, on July 25th, 1588, when the Jesuits were making determined efforts to win England back to Rome. "Two resolute Catholic gentlemen" stole and buried the remains. Here have worshipped the persecuted Presbyterians of Derby. About a century ago it was turned into dwelling-houses, and later was used as a carpenter's shop. In 1873, a Bishop's license was obtained, and once more it was used as a house of prayer. We give, by the courtesy of Mr. Richard Keene, a view of the chapel, from an interesting book published by him, in 1881, under the title of "All about Derby," by Edward Bradbury and

Richard Keene. The picture is from the pencil of the late Llewellynn Jewitt, F.S.A., the eminent antiquary.

Prior to the Reformation, the Chamberlains of Derby rendered annually to the monks of the Priory of St. James two pounds of wax, for the privilege of passing over St. James' Bridge.

On the old bridge at Rotherham, which spans the river Don, is still standing the chapel of " Our Lady."

" The sacred taper's light is gone."

It is an interesting monument of bygone times, but it is no longer used as a house of prayer. Where once the mass was celebrated by devout priests, a trader keeps a small shop. The earliest mention of this chapel which is known, occurs in the will of John Bokying, master of the Grammar School at Rotherham, and is dated August 24th, 1483. He leaves " To the fabric of the chapel to be built on Rotherham bridge, 3s. 4d." The design of the building was plain, but, on the whole, its effect must be pronounced pleasing. The dimensions of the building in the interior are thirty-two feet nine inches in length, by fifteen feet five inches in width. Leland, the antiquary, visited the town in the middle of the sixteenth

OUR LADY'S CHAPEL, ROTHERHAM BRIDGE.

century, and says, " I enterid into Rotheram by a fair stone bridge of iiij arches, and on hit is a chapel of stone, wel wrought." In old records relating to Rotherham, reproduced by John Guest, F.S.A., in his " Historic Notices of Rotherham," may be read many items of local interest on this chapel. We find statements respecting the bridge and chapel occupying the attention of the Justices of Peace at Pontefract Sessions and Doncaster Sessions, towards the close of the seventeenth century. The Feoffees of Rotherham successfully maintained that the bridge and chapel belonged to them, but that they had to be kept in repair at the expense of the West Riding. It, at this period, was used as an almshouse for poor people. In the Feoffees records it is stated as follows:

" 1778. June 6th. Ordered that the greaves do employ a proper person to examine ye state of ye almshouse, and to report what expence will be necessary to make the same into a dwelling-house for ye deputy-constable, and secure gaols for the receiption of prisoners."

" 1779. February 5th. That the greaves do immediately agree with Mr. Platts for altering the almshouse to a prison, and, according to a plan now in their hands, so that the expense of the alterations do not exceed thirty-six pounds."

" 1779. June 16th. Ordered that John Watson be permitted to inhabit that part of the alms-house designed for the deputy-constable. That the rent of the same shall be five pounds. Only to use the two first rooms and the pantry on the ground floor, and the two chambers over the same. The other parts of the house being designed for other purposes. And that he shall not take out a license to sell ale or spirituous liquors."

In 1825-6, a new court house was built, and then the bridge-chapel was no longer required as a prison. As we have previously stated, the ancient building is now devoted to business purposes. Let us hope the day is not far distant when it may once more be used as a house of prayer.

Perhaps the most interesting of chapels on bridges, is the one at Wakefield, dedicated to St. Mary. Its history has been carefully compiled by Norrisson Scatcherd, in 1843, by John W. Walker, F.S.A., in 1890, and it has received the consideration of other antiquaries. It has long been a popular, but mistaken belief, that the

chapel was built by Edward IV. that masses
might be said for those slain in the battle of
Wakefield, in 1460, and in which his father, the
Duke of York, and his brother, the

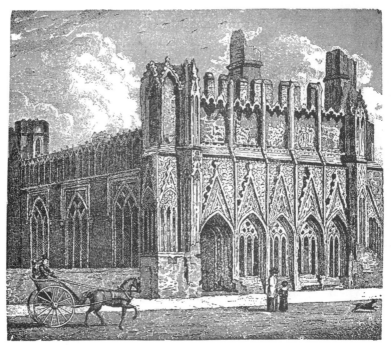

NORTH-WEST VIEW OF WAKEFIELD CHAPEL, PREVIOUS TO RE-BUILDING.

Duke of Rutland were slain. It will be
remembered, that in this engagement, the
Lancastrians defeated the Yorkists. It is clear,
from Mr. Walker's work, that the beautiful chapel
was built by the townsmen of Wakefield, and

there is not any trace of the King adding anything
to the revenues of the chapel. When the first
bridge was built over the Calder, is not known,
but, in 1342, King Edward III. granted to the
bailiffs of the town the right of tollage for three
years, on all goods for sale and cattle passing over
the bridge, "as a help towards repairing and
improving the bridge," which is stated to be
"rent and broken." In the documents, there is
not any mention of a chapel, a bridge only is
referred to. Mr. Walker is of opinion that
about this time the suggestion was first made
for the erection of a chapel in honour of the
Blessed Virgin Mary, and that it was soon carried
into effect. Three townsmen and two priests
obtained the first license, in 1356-7. In a decree,
bearing date of November 20th, 1444, it says the
chapel is "Wholly built of costly stonework by
the inhabitants and community of Wakefield."
It has been suggested that, for a time, the
black death, which caused such terrible desolation
in the country, in 1349-50, may, for a period,
have stopped the building of the chapel. It was
a noble structure when completed, the carving
being especially fine. On the west front, were
carvings representing the five glorious mysteries

of the Rosary. We give a picture of the central figures, illustrating the Resurrection. It will be seen that Christ is rising from the tomb, and on either side of him are two angels engaged in prayer. In front of the tomb are three soldiers,

SCULPTURE IN THE CENTRAL COMPARTMENT OF THE WEST FRONT.

placed there as guards, and they are clad in complete armour of the time of Edward III. An important feature of the Wakefield bridge-chapel is the crypt. "This," says Scatcherd, "has undoubtedly been the dwelling of the priests— where they might have lodged strangers, or administered relief." There was a high turret, reached by a little spiral staircase. On this elevated part of the building was kindled the cresset-light, which would guide the wayfarer, and possibly assist the navigator on the river Calder, when day had given way to night.

NORTH-EAST VIEW OF WAKEFIELD BRIDGE-CHAPEL, 1810.

The chapel was for many years used for secular purposes, but, happily, opened for public worship on Easter Sunday, April 22nd, 1848. It had been previously rebuilt by Mr. G. G. Scott, and the west front is still to be seen at Kettlethorpe

Hall, and forms the front of a boathouse. The rebuilding, instead of restoring, was a serious mistake. The Bath and Caen stone used does not resist the wasting action of the impurities in the air. " It was in an evil hour," says Scott, "that I yielded, and allowed a new front in Caen stone, in place of the weather-beaten old one. . . . I never repented it but once, that has been ever since. . . . I think of this with the utmost shame and chagrin." We state, on the authority of Mr. Walker, that, " Sir Gilbert Scott, some years before his death, was so anxious to have the old front replaced in its original position, that he offered to contribute freely towards this object, if he could persuade the Yorkshire people to help him, but nothing further was done."

## Charter Horns.

IN the Cathedrals of York and Carlisle are preserved interesting charter horns. The horn, in bygone times, often played an important part when land was granted. In some instances ancient drinking horns are the only charters proving the ownership of extensive possessions. The blowing of the horn has formed, and still forms, the prelude of many quaint customs for maintaining certain manorial and other rights. Some of the details of the old services of manors are extremely romantic, and supply not a few strange chapters in local and national history. Romance, in some of the records, takes the place of dry matter-of-fact statements, and adds not a little to the pleasure of the study of past ages.

The important Horn of Ulphus is preserved in the treasure room of York Minster, and, apart

from its rich historical associations, it is an
object of great beauty. It is made from a
portion of a large tusk of an elephant. Were
this horn totally without a history or a tradition
connected with it, its elaborate and peculiar
character of ornamentation would render it an
object of interest and value. It has two bands,
one near the thinner end and the other at about
a fifth part of the length from the thicker end.
The space between the latter band and the end

THE HORN OF ULPHUS.

is adorned with sculptures in low relief, which
express much that in European mediæval art
did not appear for several hundreds of years
later than the date of the horn, and which,
it may fairly be supposed, are of Asiatic origin.
The band of carvings is about four inches in
width, and there are four chief figures. One
appears to be an unicorn performing the act
that, in the credulous natural history of long ago,
it was so apt to indulge—namely, piercing a tree

with its one horn, and so fixing itself and being at the hunter's mercy. The unicorn is the symbol of chastity. At the other side of the tree is a lion killing and devouring a deer. Next, facing another tree with palmated leaves and grape-like fruit, is a gryphon, a creature having the body of a lion and the head and wings of an eagle. At the other side of this tree, and facing the gryphon, is a similar monster, which has, however, the head of a dog or wolf. The lion's tail is foliated, while those of the winged beasts end in ludicrous dogs' or wolves' heads. Three wolves' heads, collared, rise from the ground-line, and a wolf runs in the upper part, and it is not unlikely that Ulphus (or Ulf, equal to our word wolf) is so hinted at. The form of the animals, especially those which have wings, are Assyrian in feeling and treatment, while the treatment of the trees still further adds to the opinion that the horn is not a specimen of European carving.

Mr. Robert Davies, F.S.A., Town-Clerk of York, who wrote a monograph on this celebrated relic, from which a few of our particulars are drawn, conjectures that the horn would be brought to the Baltic shores by Arabic merchants ; if so, it will be then more feasible to

suppose that the carving would be executed
previous to its being brought for sale. Having
so far considered the form of the horn, let us next
look a little into its history. The tradition,
accepted from time immemorial, is simply this—
that, a considerable period before the Conquest,
the horn was given to the see of York by a Dane
who had settled in England, as a symbol of
endowment of the wide lands which he conferred
upon the episcopate. This tradition comes down
to the present day through various channels.
First is a poem in Latin (among the Cotton
MSS.), describing the different gifts to York up
to about the twelfth century. In this, Ulf is
described as an eminent Yorkshire earl and ruler,
his gifts to the church are mentioned, and their
confirmation by Edward the Confessor, the horn
is noted to be the sign of endowment, and its
great beauty enlarged upon. In one particular,
the description differs from one that might be
written at the present day, inasmuch that,
whereas the horn is stated in the poem to be
white, its hue now is brown. In Holland's
" Britannia," the tradition is given as historically
true, and in the following words : " Then it was,
also, that princes bestowed many great livings

and lands upon the church of York, especially Ulphus, the son of Torald (I note so much out of an old book, that there may plainly appear a custom of our ancestors in endowing churches with livings). This Ulphus, aforesaid, ruled the west part of Deira, and by reason of the debate that was like to arise between his sons, the younger and the elder, about their lordships and their seigniories after his death, forthwith he made them all alike. For, without delay, he went to York, took the horn with him out of which he was wont to drink, filled it with wine, and, before the altar of God, blessed Saint Peter, prince of the Apostles, kneeling upon his knees, he drank, and thereby enfeoffed them [the church] in all his lands and revenues. Which horn was there kept, as a monument (as I have heard) until our fathers' days."

In Domesday Book is mentioned an English thane named Ulf, who, in the reign of Edward the Confessor, had held large possessions in Northumbria, which, at the time of the Domesday Survey, had become the property of the see of York. It is further stated, that large territories which were held by the Archbishop of York, at the time of the Conquest, had also been owned by this same

Ulf. In Kirkby's "Inquest" (*temp.* Edward I.), these lands are again noted to be the gift of Ulf. Thus far, the tradition is corroborated by history, but the statement that Ulf's sons were disinherited is incorrect, for Ulf had a large extent of property left after making his munificent gift to the Church, which his sons in due time inherited. These two sons, Archil and Norman, are included among the King's thanes in Domesday Book. There was also another Ulf, who

THE PUSEY HORN.

lived in the time of the King Canute, dying in 1036, but, though confounded with the Ulphus of our story, he was not the same, and had nothing to do with the charter horn of York.

The Pusey Horn, preserved at Pusey House, near Farringdon, has a curious traditional history, carrying us back to the days of the warlike Canute, and his struggles with the Saxons. It is related, that, on one occasion, the king's soldiers and the Saxons were encamped near each other, in the neighbourhood of Pusey. An ancestor of the Pusey family, serving as an officer under the king, discovered an ambuscade, formed by the Saxons, to intercept the king's army. He gave Canute a timely intimation of their intentions, and thus enabled him to foil their plans. For this important information, Canute gave to his informant and his heirs the manor of Pusey, and as a ratification of the grant, a horn was presented. It is the horn of an ox, measuring two feet and half-an-inch in length, and at the larger end is a foot in circumference. The colour of it is dark brown. Round the middle is a ring of silver-gilt, and the horn is supported on two hound's feet. The small end has a screw stopper, also of silver-gilt, in the form of a hound's head. It forms with the stopper a drinking horn, and without it a hunting horn. The silver ring bears the following inscription :

Hickes, writing about 1685, states : " Both the horn and manor were in his time possessed by Charles Pusey, who had recovered them in Chancery, before Lord Chancellor Jefferies ; the horn itself being produced in court, and with universal admiration received, admitted, and proved to be the identical horn by which, as by charter, Canute had conveyed the manor of Pusey about seven hundred years before." On the 25th of October, 1849, at a festival at Wantage, Berkshire, to celebrate the anniversary of the birthday of King Alfred, a dinner was held, and amongst the guests were Mr. Pusey, M.P., John Britton, the antiquary, and other notable men. It is reported that, "during the proceedings, a pleasureable interest was excited by the production of the extraordinary piece of antiquity, the Pusey Horn, presented by King Canute to the ancestor of Mr. Pusey, and forming the original tenure of the Pusey property, and inalienable from it."

According to a popular legend, Edward the Confessor presented to a huntsman named Nigel, and his heirs, a hide of land and a wood called Hulewood, and the rangership of the royal forest of Bernwood, Buckinghamshire, as a reward for

his courage in slaying a large wild boar which
infested the place. The land was called
Derehyde, and on it he built a house, naming it
Borestalle, in memory of the slain animal. The
grant was accompanied with a horn, which is
preserved by the lords of Borestalle, and is
known as Nigel's horn. It is described as
"being of a dark-brown colour, variegated and
veined like tortoise-shell, and fitted with straps of
leather to hang about the neck. It is tipped at
each end with silver-gilt, and mounted with a
plate of brass, having sculptured thereon the
figure of a horn, and also several plates of silver-
gilt *fleurs-de-lis*, and an old brass seal ring." In
addition to the horn, is also preserved, an old
folio vellum volume, containing transcripts of
charters and evidences relating to the estate. It
contains, we read, a rude drawing of the site of
Borstall House and Manor, and under is the rude
figure of a man presenting, on his knees, to the
king, the head of a boar, on the point of a sword,
and the king returning to him a coat-of-arms,
arg. a fesse, gu. two crescents, and a horn, verde.
The armorial bearings belong to a much later
period than the reign of Edward the Confessor.

Before the Rhyne Toll was collected in Buck-

inghamshire, a horn was blown with not a little
ceremony.  The right of gathering the toll
originated as a reward for a heroic deed performed in the days when the wild boar roamed
the forests of England, much to the terror of the
people.  According to tradition, a ferocious boar
had its lair in the ancient forest of Rookwoode.
It kept the inhabitants of the district in constant
fear of their lives, and prevented strangers visiting
them.  A valiant knight, the Lord of Chetwode,
resolved to rid the country of the monster, or die
in the attempt.  Says an old ballad :

" Then he blowed a blast full north, south, east, and west—
    Wind well thy horn, good hunter ;
And the wild boar then heard him full in his den,
    As he was a jovial hunter.

Then he made the best of his speed unto him—
    Wind well thy horn, good hunter ;
Swift flew the boar, with his tusks smeared with gore,
    To Sir Ryalas, the jovial hunter.

Then the wild boar, being so stout and so strong—
    Wind well thy horn, good hunter ;
Thrashed down the trees as he ramped him along
    To Sir Ryalas, the jovial hunter.

Then they fought four hours on a long summer day—
    Wind well thy horn, good hunter ;
Till the wild boar would fain have got him away
    From Sir Ryalas, the jovial hunter.

"Then Sir Ryalas he drawed his broad sword with might—
    Wind well thy horn, good hunter;
And he fairly cut the boar's head off quite,
    For he was a jovial hunter."

The countryside rang with the knight's praise, and the king heard the welcome news. The sovereign, as a reward for his services, made "the jovial hunter," we are told, "the knight tenant *in capite*, and constituted his manor paramount of all the manors within the limits and extent of the royal forest of Rookwoode." The privilege of levying toll on all cattle passing through nine townships was granted to him and his heirs for ever. It was known as the Rhyne Toll, and commenced at midnight on October 29th, and ended at midnight on November 7th annually. Before the commencement of the collection of the toll, a horn was blown, as we have previously stated, with some ceremony. The toll was collected until 1868, when it was given up by Sir George Chetwode, the lord of the manor.

In the Chapter House, at Carlisle, is preserved an interesting relic known as the "Horns of the Altar." Mr. Frank Buckland inspected it in 1879, and expressed his astonishment at finding it to be a walrus's skull, without the lower jaw, with tusks about eighteen inches long. The skull itself was marked out with faded colours, so as to somewhat resemble a human skull. Canon Prescott supplied Mr. Buckland with some information about this curious charter horn. He said : " In the year 1290, a claim was made by the King, Edward I., and by others, to the tithes on certain lands lately brought under cultivation in the forest of Inglewood. The Prior of Carlisle appeared on behalf of his convent, and urged their right to the property on the ground that the tithes had been granted to them by a former king, who had enfeoffed them by a certain ivory horn (*quoddam cornu eburneum*), which he gave to the Church of Carlisle, and which they possessed at that time. The Cathedral of Carlisle has had in its possession for a great number of years two fine walrus tusks, with a portion of the skull. They appear in ancient inventories of goods of the cathedral as 'one horn of the altar, in two parts,' or 'two horns of the altar' (1674), to-gether with other articles of the altar furniture. But antiquaries come to the conclusion that these were identical with the 'ivory horn' referred to above. Communications were made to the Society of Antiquaries (see *Archæologia*, Vol. III.) and they were called the 'Carlisle Charter

Horns.' Such charter horns were not uncommon in ancient days. Bishop Lyttleton (1768), in a paper read before the society, said the 'horns' were so called improperly, being 'certainly the teeth of some very large sea fish.' It is probable that they were presented to the church as an offering, perhaps by some traveller, and used as an ornament to the altar. Such ornaments were frequent, both at the smaller altars and in the churches."

Mr. Buckland, adverting to the foregoing, says : " I cannot quite understand how a walrus's skull and teeth came to be considered so valuable as to be promoted to the dignity of a charter horn of a great cathedral like Carlisle. I am afraid Bishop Lyttleton, 1768, was not a naturalist, or he would never have called the tusks of a walrus ' the teeth of some very large fish.' "

Hungerford, a pretty little town at the extreme west end of the royal county of Berks, has its ancient charter horn, and linked to it are some curious customs. A contributor to a local journal for 1876, states that "the town of Hungerford, Berkshire, enjoys some rare privileges and maintains some quaint customs. The inhabitants have the right of pasturage and of shooting over a

large tract of downs and marsh land bequeathed
to them by John of Gaunt, Duke of Lancaster,
subject to the annual observance of certain
customs at this period of the year. They have
also the right of fishing for trout in the Kennet,
which flows through the borough. Hockney-day
and the usual customs have just been observed
in their integrity. The old horn, by which the
tenure is held, had been blown from the Town
Hall, summoning the commoners to their rights,
and the tything men, whose duties are unique,
have ably fulfilled them. These gentlemen carry
long poles, decorated with flowers and garlands,
having to call at each house and exact the tribute
of a coin from each male, and a kiss from each
lady. The High Constable or Mayor, whose
office combines the duties of the coroner, is chosen
on this day."

Blowing three blasts on a horn formed part of
an old custom at Chingford, Essex. Blount, in
his " Tenures of Land," and the historians of the
county, direct attention to the ceremony. The
estate of Brindwood's was held under the
following conditions : Upon every alteration,
the owner of the estate, with his wife, man
servant, and maid servant, each single on a

horse, come to the parsonage, where the owner does his homage, and pays his relief in the manner following—he blows three blasts with his horn, carries a hawk on his fist, and his servant has a greyhound in a slip, both for the use of the rector for the day ; he receives a chicken for his hawk, a peck of oats for his horse, and a loaf of bread for his greyhound. They all dine, after which the master blows three blasts with his horn, and they all depart. A correspondent to the *Gentleman's Magazine* for 1790, gives particulars of this custom being kept up in the days of Queen Elizabeth.

At Bainbridge, the chief place of the forest of Wensleydale, Yorkshire, still lingers an old horn-blowing custom. An instrument known as the forest horn is blown on the green every night at ten o'clock from the first of September to Shrovetide. It is a very large one, and made from the horn of an ox. Its sound on the still night air may be heard for a considerable distance. In bygone ages, horns were blown to enable belated travellers to direct their course over the almost trackless roads to their destinations, and the welcome notes of the horn have saved many a lonely wayfarer from perishing in the snow.

SUNDAY IN THE OLDEN TIME.

## The Old English Sunday.

THE history of Sunday in England is a subject which merits careful consideration. The laws and customs of bygone times are both curious and interesting. The manner of observing Sunday is a subject which is fast coming to the front, and one which we must be prepared to discuss in a spirit of fairness.

In our investigations we shall find that, prior to the period of the Puritans coming into power in England, the day did not rank higher than other festivals observed by the Church.

Our Sunday laws commence with the Saxons, a rude race, who delighted in a wild life, in which war and bloodshed formed prominent features. Gluttony and drunkenness prevailed to a considerable extent.

The laws and canons passed from the

G

days of Ine, who commenced to reign in Wessex
in the year 688, to the time of Edward the
Confessor, who died in 1066, clearly show that
the Saxon rulers did their utmost to prevent
Sunday labour, and that firm measures were also
taken to put a stop to marketing on that day.

It appears, from the enactments of Ine, that if
a lord commanded his slave to work on a Sunday,
the slave became a freeman, and the lord was
also fined thirty shillings. If, unknown to his
lord, a slave worked, he was severely punished,
or, in lieu of corporal punishment, he had to pay
a fine. If a freeman was found guilty of Sunday
labour, he had to forfeit his freedom, or pay a fine
of sixty shillings. A priest was doubly liable.

Alfred was King of Wessex from 871 to 901,
and we learn from his laws that if a thief was
caught stealing on Sunday, at Yule, at Easter, on
Holy Thursday, or during Rogation days, the
penalty was double the amount of fine inflicted
during the Lenten fast.

The laws of Edward, the elder, and Guthrum,
made after the peace between the Danes and the
English, 901 to 924, include some strict Sunday
regulations. "If any one engage in Sunday
marketing," says the statute, "let him forefit the

chattel, and twelve ore (192 pence) among the Danes, and thirty shillings among the English." King Athelstan, about 924, passed a similar act to the preceding one, anent Sunday marketing.

Several important ecclesiastical laws were made in the reign of Edgar, which commenced in 959 and ended 975. We find, according to his enactments, that Sunday was to be kept from noontide on Saturday until the dawn of Monday, on peril of a fine. The following are two of his canons :

"And we enjoin you, that on feast days, heathen songs and devil's games be abstained from."

"And we enjoin, that Sunday and folk-motes be abstained from."

When Canute, King of Denmark, became King of England, he passed several laws similar to those of Edgar. He also directed that Sunday should commence at noon on Saturday and end at dawn on Monday. He strongly forbade marketing and worldly works on Sunday. A condemned man in this reign was not put to death on a Sunday, unless he commenced fighting or attempted to flee.

Before leaving this section of our subject, it

may be observed that the settlement of the Danes here did not produce any great changes, for the customs and institutions of their native land were similar to those of England. The civilization of the Danes, however, was lower in its standard than that of the Saxons. During the whole of the Anglo-Saxon period, slaves were sold like cattle in the open market. Many slaves were exported to Scotland and Ireland from the English markets.

It may not be out of place to make a few remarks on slavery. They have not any special bearing on the Sunday question, but illustrate the hard life of the period when severe laws prevailed. Of circumstances which brought persons into slavery, we may mention, in the first place, those obtained by right of conquest; next, those sold into slavery by their parents or by their own free will; another class were those found guilty of stealing, who were made slaves as a punishment for their crimes; many were doomed to slavery through not being able to pay the penalties imposed for breaking the laws of the land; and lastly, we find not a few traces of men voluntarily surrendering their liberty for food. Famines, at this time, occurred very often, and men were glad to be slaves for their own daily bread. A parent might sell his child if it had reached the age of seven years, and at thirteen a child might sell itself into slavery. A slave was usually estimated at four times the value of an ox. In the reign of King Athelstan, the punishment for theft was most severe; and, on the authority of Lingard, it is stated that a law was made respecting the offences committed by slaves against others than their masters, to the effect that a man thief was ordered to be stoned to death by twenty of his fellows, each of whom was punished with three whippings if he failed thrice to hit the culprit. A woman thief was burnt by eighty women slaves, each of whom brought three billets of wood to the execution. If she failed, she was likewise subjected to the punishment of three whippings. After the death of the offender, each slave paid three pennies as a fine to the proprietor. As Christianity spread, the condition of the slave became happier than before its truths were known. The slave might still be sold at the pleasure of the owner, but with the important restriction that a Christian was not permitted to be made over to a Pagan.

A low value was set on human life in Saxon

England. Flogging was generally adopted for punishing persons guilty of offences, whether slight or serious. It was not an uncommon practice for mistresses to whip, or have their servants whipped to death.

On the 14th of October, in the year 1066, was fought the battle of Hastings. The contending armies were one led by Harold, the last of the Saxon kings, and the other by William, Duke of Normandy. Harold was slain, his brave followers defeated, and on the following Christmas Day, in the Abbey of Westminster, the Conqueror was crowned William I. On the whole, he made a noble sovereign, and the Normans added nobility of character to the people of the country in which they settled. It may fairly be asserted that all that is best of old English life is the outcome of the settlement of the Normans in this land. The Sunday laws under the Normans were, to a large extent, an expansion of those in force in the Saxon era. Sunday trading received much attention, several enactments being passed respecting it. In earlier ages, markets and fairs were held on a Sunday, and in many instances in churchyards. At the commencement of the fourteenth century, the traders of Cockermouth suffered much from the active business operations at Crosthwaite. A petition was presented to Parliament, in 1305, by the inhabitants of the former town, stating that, owing to the sale of corn, flour, beans, flesh, fish, and other kinds of merchandise at Crosthwaite Church, on Sundays, their market was fast declining, and that the persons who farmed the tolls from the king were unable to pay their rent. An order was made for closing the church market at Crosthwaite.

Thursday was the chartered market-day at Bradford, Yorkshire, but it was changed to Sunday, and doubtless was held in the church-yard. The toll, about the time of Edward I., it is said, yielded £3 per annum, an amount equal to about £45 of money at the present time.

A statute, made in the reign of Edward I., in the year 1285, ordered "that, from henceforth, neither fairs nor markets be held in churchyards, for the honour of the Church."

A market was granted to the town of Sedge-field, Durham, by Bishop Kellawe, in the year 1312, and it was to be held on a Friday. The people soon brought about a change, and held the market on a Sunday. The rector of Sedgefield directed the attention of Bishop Bury to the Sunday trading, and he confirmed the grant made a few years previously.

John Thorsby, Archbishop of York, about the year 1367, delivered to his subordinates a charge respecting Sunday trading. It is stated in the document as follows: "Desiring, therefore, to obviate some errors and abuses, so far as we can, which we see to grow rife in the church; in the first place (according to the example of Christ, who would have his own church called a house, not of merchandise, but of prayer; and not allowing fraudulent traffic there to be exercised, cast the buyers and sellers out of the temple), we firmly forbid any one to keep a market in the churches, the porches, and cemeteries thereunto belonging, or other holy places of our diocese, on the Lord's day or other festivals, or to presume to traffic or hold any secular pleasures therein; and let there be no wrestlings, shootings, or plays, which may be the cause of sin, dissension, hatred, or fighting, therein performed; but let every Catholic come thither to pray, and to implore pardon for his sin." About this time, a similar charge was made by the Archbishop of Canterbury.

In the year 1409, a statute of Henry IV. ordered :

" He that playeth at unlawful games on Sundays and other festival days prohibited by the statute, shall be six days imprisoned."

At Hull, in 1428, the local bench of magistrates drew up a code of regulations respecting Sunday trading. The chief orders were as follow :

" That no markets be held upon Sunday, nor any merchandise or goods sold thereon, under penalty of 6s. 8d. to the seller and 3s. 4d. to the buyer, except according to ancient custom, from Lammas to Michaelmas."

" That no butcher sell or expose for sale any meat on Sunday, under the aforesaid penalty."

" That no cooks nor victuallers dress any meat on Sunday, except for strangers, and that, too, before eleven o'clock."

" That no tradesmen keep their shops open on Sunday, nor sell any goods ; nor any vintners or ale-sellers deliver or sell ale or wine on Sunday, under the aforesaid penalties."

" Any person who shall inform against transgressors, shall be entitled to one-eighth over and above half of the sums so forfeited, provided he acted out of pure zeal, devoid of self-interest or malice."

The City Records of Worcester contain some quaint items on the observance of Sunday. We may infer from a regulation made by the local authorities, at the commencement of the reign of Queen Elizabeth, that the laws were not very stringent respecting Sunday trading. It was resolved that the shopkeepers were to open "only one top window on a Sunday." "This was," to use the words of a local historian, "a decided case of huckstership dividing its affection between God and Mammon."

The strangest circumstances anent Sunday trading remain to be told, and belong to the days of Charles II. It is stated on reliable authority, that a meat market was held at Wigton, Cumberland, on a Sunday, and that the butchers suspended carcases of meat at the church door, to attract the attention of persons attending divine service. "It was," says the writer from whom we glean these particulars, "even no uncommon thing for people who had made their bargains before the service, to hang their joints of meat over the backs of their seats until the ceremony was concluded." The practice was so distasteful to the priest, that, being unable to prevent it, he made a journey to London on foot, with a petition to the king to alter the market day to Tuesday, a request which was readily granted.

Sunday trading prevailed for a long period. Adam Clarke was appointed to preach in the Norfolk circuit in 1783, and he says here "multitudes, even those called religious people, bought and sold without any remorse."

It was the common practice in country districts, even down to the commencement of the nineteenth century, for the parish clerk, on a Sunday morning, to mount a grave stone, and for the worshippers to gather round him and listen to the announcements of coming auction sales, particulars of rewards offered for the conviction of persons who had been guilty of trespassing and committing wilful damage in the district—indeed, all kinds of workaday matters were made known. Some of the old parish accounts contain references to payments made to the parish clerks for services rendered. It appears from the accounts of Newchurch, Rossendale, that the parish clerk stood in his desk in the church, and gave out secular notices, in which the people were supposed to take an interest. There is a legend still lingering in the district, that bull-baitings were amongst the matters proclaimed by the parish clerk of this church. The church accounts state under the year 1804 :

"Parish Clerk in giving Public

Notices in the Church.........o  2  6."

At Ravenstonedale, when the practice of announcing sales, etc., in the churchyard ceased, the attendance at the ancient parish church diminished. The old parish clerks made many amusing blunders when giving out the public notices, and the following illustration may be given as an example. We are told that he was instructed to make known a change of service, as follows : "On Sunday next, the service in this church will be held in the afternoon, and on the following Sunday, it will be held in the morning, and so on alternately until further notice." Instead of delivering the preceding notice, he said : "On Sunday next, the morning service in this church will be held in the afternoon, and on the following Sunday, the afternoon service will be held in the morning, and so on to all eternity."

In the days of yore, stage plays were performed on Sunday, not only in the churches, but in the theatres. Old church accounts contain may items bearing on plays in parish churches. The books of St. Martin's, Leicester, state :

" 1560. Pd. to the plears for their
    paynes .................................vij.d."

The Bewdley chapel-wardens' accounts for the year 1572, includes a disbursement as follows :

" Paid unto the quenes plaiers in the
    church ...............................6s. 8d."

The Corporation of Lyme, in 1558, paid 4s. 5d. to the Queen's players, who performed in the parish church. "We may suppose," says Mr. George Roberts in his "Social History," "that money was taken at the doors by some official of the mayor, who ascertained the deficiency to be as above." The Syston registers state :

" 1602. Paid to Lord Morden's
    players, because they should not
    play in the church...................xij.d."

Prior to this period, not a few attempts had been made to stop acting in churches. Bonner, Bishop of London, issued, in 1542, a proclamation to the clergy in his diocese, prohibiting "all manner of common plays, games, or interludes to be played, set forth, or declared within their churches or chapels." The author of a tract, published in 1572, writes strongly respecting the clergy neglecting their duty, and adverts to acting in churches. Speaking of the clergyman conducting the service, the writer says : " He againe posteth it over as fast as he can gallop ; for he either hath two places to serve, or else there are some games to be played in the afternoon, as lying the whetstone, heathenish dancing of the ring, a beare or bull to be bayted, or else jack-an-apes to ryde on horse back, or an enterlude to be played ; and if no place else can be gotten, it must be done in the church."

Two companies of players, in 1539, visited Knowsley ; one was the Queen's players, and the other the Earl of Essex's players. On the Sunday after their arrival, the rector of Standish preached in the morning, the Queen's players acted in the afternoon, and the Earl's players at night. Other Sunday performances were given in the district by the actors at this time.

Before 1579, Sunday appears to have been the only day upon which plays were performed, but after that year they were acted on other days as well as on Sunday. It was not the fashion for females to visit theatres, but at Oxford we find that Queen Elizabeth witnessed a Sunday theatrical exhibition. James I., at his Court on a

Sunday, had plays provided. The Bishop of Lincoln, on Sunday night, September 27th, 1631, had performed, in his London house, the play of "A Midsummer Night's Dream," and for this he was indicted by the Puritans. Masques on a Sunday night at this period were extremely popular.

During a visit of James I. to Oxford, in 1621, on a Sunday in August, the university men produced a piece called the "Marriage of Arts." It was not a successful entertainment, the king and his friends failing to appreciate the wit of the undergraduates. Says an epigram of the period:

"At Christ Church, 'Marriage' done before the King,
Least that some mates should want an offering,
The King himself did offer—what, I pray?
He offered twice or thrice to go away."

In the town of Hull, the player, about this period, does not appear to have been regarded with much esteem. The earliest notice of theatres in Hull occurs in the year 1598, and we learn from Mr. Sheahan, the local historian: "That the Mayor issued an order, in which 'divers idle, lewd persons, players, or setters of plays, tragedies, comedies, and interludes,' who were in the habit of coming to the town, were denounced." In this document, it was further set

forth that persons patronising their performances would have to forfeit 2s. 6d. for every
offence.

Football was introduced into England by the
Romans, and it is our oldest sport. In past ages,
it was a popular Sunday amusement, and, in not
a few places, it was played until the earlier years
of the present century. Attempts were made to
prevent its being practised during the time of
Divine service. An entry bearing on this subject
appears in the parish accounts of Colne, Lancashire. The item is as follows :

" 1713. My charges with ye
men taken playing at football
in ye tyme of Divine servis
to ye Justice.................... oo oi oo."

The local authorities were equally severe on
Sunday idlers. The accounts for the year 1737
include a charge " for warrant to take up idle
persons on the Sabbath-day, £0 2s. od." An
annual football match was formerly played at
Beverley on the Sunday preceding the races.
The game commenced on the racecourse, and
was attended by a large number of persons from
the surrounding villages. The Corporation made
several attempts to stop the custom, but without

avail until 1825, and then not without a struggle. A number of constables received special instructions to stop the sport, but they were, however, severely handled, and the match was played. The aggressors were subsequently tried, and convicted of assault, and imprisoned with hard labour for a time. This action prevented any further Sunday football playing at Beverley.

A good anecdote is related in Dawson's "History of Skipton," respecting Sunday football playing. It is stated that the Rev. J. Alcock, B.A., of Burnsall, was on his way to conduct afternoon service, when he saw a number of boys playing football. "With a solemn shake of the head," says Mr. Dawson, "he rebuked them. 'This is very wrong, you are breaking the Sabbath!' The remonstrance fell unheeded, and the next moment the ball rolled to Mr. Alcock's feet. He gave a tremendous kick, sending it high in the air. 'That's the way to play football!' he said to the ring of admiring athletes, and then, amidst their universal praise, he proceeded on his way to church."

Bowling was, in bygone ages, a popular Sunday pastime. Ladies appear to have greatly enjoyed the sport. Charles I. and Archbishop

H

Laud were both very fond of bowling. When Laud was taken to task for playing on Sunday, he defended himself by showing that it was well known to be one of the favourite amusements of the Church of Geneva. When John Knox, the Scottish reformer, visited Calvin, he arrived on a Sunday, and found Calvin enjoying a game at bowls. It is not stated if Knox joined in the pastime, but we certainly know that he travelled, wrote letters, and even entertained Ambassadors and others on this day. On a Sunday, in the year 1562, Knox attended the marriage of James Stuart (afterwards the Earl of Murray), and it is asserted that he countenanced a display which included a banquet, a marquee, dancing, fireworks, etc. Not a few of the godly lifted up their voices in condemnation, not so much, we infer, on account of the day, but the extravagances to which the amusements were carried. About half a century later, was married, on Shrove Sunday, 1613, Frederick, the Prince Palatine, and the Princess Elizabeth. The day ended, we are told, according to the custom of such assemblies, with dancing, masking, and revelling. In the works of Shakespeare and other dramatists will be found many allusions to Sunday weddings.

We gather from numerous Acts of Parliament, and other sources, that, after attending church, the people in the old days devoted themselves to "honest recreation and manly sports." Particular attention was paid to the practice of archery. Richard II., for example, in the year 1388, directed that his subjects, who were servants of husbandry, and artificers, should use the bow on Sundays and other holidays, and they were enjoined to give up "tennis, football, dice, casting the stone, and other importune games." The next king, Henry IV., strictly enforced the statute made by his predecessor, and those who infringed it were liable to be imprisoned for six days.

Sunday was a great day for bear baiting. It was on the last Sunday of April, 1520, that part of the chancel of St. Mary's Church, Beverley, fell, killing fifty-five people, who had assembled for the celebration of mass. A bear baiting, held in another part of the town, at the same time, had drawn a much greater crowd together, and hence the origin of the Yorkshire saying, "It is better to be at the baiting of a bear, than the singing of a mass." At an accident in a London bear-garden, the people did not fare so well, for we learn that on a "Sunday afternoon, in the year 1582, the scaffolds being overcharged with spectators, fell during the performance, and a great number of persons were killed or maimed by the accident."

We get a good idea of the Sunday amusements in vogue at the time of Elizabeth, from a license the Queen granted to a poor man, permitting him to provide for the public certain Sunday sports. "To all mayors, sheriffs, constables, and other head officers within the county of Middlesex.— After our hearty commendations, whereas we are informed that one John Seconton, poulter, dwelling within the parish of St. Clement's Danes, being a poor man, having four small children, and fallen into decay, is licensed to have and use some plays and games at or upon several Sundays, for his better relief, comfort, and sustentation, within the county of Middlesex, to commence and begin at and from the 22nd of May next coming, after the date hereof, and not to remain in one place above three several Sundays ; and we, considering that great resort of people is like to come thereunto, we will and require of you, as well for good order, as also for the preservation of the Queen's Majesty's peace, that you take with you four or five of the discreet and substantial men within

your office or liberties where the games shall be
put in practice, then and there to foresee and do
your endeavour to your best in that behalf, during
the continuance of the games or plays, which
games are hereafter severally mentioned; that is
to say, the shooting with the standard, the
shooting with the broad arrow, the shooting at
twelve score prick, the shooting at the Turk, the
leaping for men, the running for men, the
wrestling, the throwing of the sledge, and the
pitching of the bar, with all such other games as
have at any time heretofore or now be licensed,
used, or played. Given the 26th day of April,
in the eleventh year of the Queen's Majesty's
reign."—[1569.]

The Puritans were making their power felt
early in the seventeenth century, and doing their
utmost to curtail Sunday amusements. The
history of the north of England supplies not a
few facts bearing on this matter. One illustration
we may give you as an instance of many which
might be mentioned. Elias Micklethwaite filled
the office of chief magistrate of York, in the year
1615, and during his mayoralty, he attempted to
enforce a strict observance of the Sabbath.
During the Sunday, he kept closed the city gates,

and thus prevented the inhabitants from going into the country for pleasure.

Speaking of city gates, we are reminded of the fact that great precaution used to be taken against the Scotch in the North of England. Many were the battles between the men of England and Scotland. A Scotchman was not formerly permitted to enter the city of York without a license from the Lord Mayor, the Warden, or the Constable, on pain of imprisonment. In 1501, hammers were placed on each of the bars for Scotchmen to knock before entering.

To return to Sunday amusements, James I., in the year 1617, coming from Scotland to London, passed through Lancashire, and was received with every token of loyalty. He was entertained at Hoghton Tower in a manner befitting a monarch. It is not without interest to state how the king and his suite spent the Sunday at this stronghold on the 17th August, 1617. A sermon was first preached by Bishop Morton; next, dinner was served, which was of a substantial character. About four o'clock, a rush-bearing, preceded by "piping," was witnessed by the king. After the rustic merriment, the company partook of supper, which was almost as formidable as the dinner. After supper, the king repaired to the garden, and a masque of noblemen, knights, and gentlemen passed before him. Speeches were made, and lastly, the night was concluded by " dancing the Huckler, Tom Bedlo, and the cowp Justice of the Peace." It is stated that Bishop Morton condemned the profaneness of the company who had disturbed the service at the church. During the king's visit to the country, it is recorded that a large number of the tradesmen, peasants, and servants, of the County Palatine, presented a petition, praying that they might be permitted to have the old out-door pastimes after the services at the church were over. The king granted their request, and issued a proclamation from his palace, at Greenwich, on May 24th, 1618, sanctioning various sports after divine service on Sunday. It was meant only for Lancashire. The recreations named are dancing, archery, leaping, vaulting, May games, Witsun-ales, morris-dancers, and setting up of May-poles. The document, known as the " Book of Sports," gave considerable offence to the Puritans. Clergymen were directed to read it in their churches.

The question came forward under the next

king, Charles I., and on October 18th, 1633, he ratified and published his father's declaration. This action, in many quarters, was most displeasing, and a number of the clergy refused to read the order. One of the ministers was, in 1637, deprived and excommunicated by the High Commission Court for not acceding to the request. Six years later, namely, in 1643, the Lords and Commons ordered the " Book of Sports " to be burned by the common hangman, at Cheapside and other public places.

We have now brought down our investigations to the days of the Commonwealth. King Charles's life closed in a tragic manner, at the hands of the headsman, on a scaffold erected before one of the windows of the Palace of Whitehall. Old times are changed, and old manners gone ; a stranger fills the Stuart throne. In our pity for unfortunate Charles, we must not forget that English life under the Stuarts became demoralised, the court setting a baneful example, which the people were not slow to follow. Licentiousness and blasphemy were mistaken for signs of gentility, and little regard was paid to virtue. Debauchery was general, and at the festive seasons was carried to an alarming extent.

The Puritans, with all their faults, and it must be admitted that their faults were many, had a regard for sound Christian principles ; and the prevailing lack of reverence for virtue, morality, and piety, was most distasteful to them, and caused them to try to put an end to the follies and vices of the age.

Various Acts of Parliament were passed to check work and amusement on the Lord's Day. We get from the Puritans our present manner of observing Sunday. The following are a few extracts from the " Directory of Public Prayers, reading of the Holy Scriptures," etc., which was adopted by the Puritan Parliament in 1644. It is therein stated :

" The Lord's Day ought to be so remembered beforehand, as that all worldly business of our ordinary callings may be so ordered, and so timely and seasonably laid aside, as they may not be impediments to the due sanctifying of the day when it comes.

The whole day is to be celebrated as holy to the Lord, both in public and in private, as being the Christian Sabbath, to which ends it is requisite that there be a holy cessation or resting all the day, from all unnecessary labour, and an abstaining not only from all sports and pastimes, but also from all worldly words and thoughts.

That the diet on that day be so ordered as that neither servants be unnecessarily detained from the public worship of God, nor any other persons hindered from sanctifying that day.

That there be private preparation of every person and family by prayer for themselves, for God's assistance of the minister, and for a blessing upon the ministry, and by such other holy exercises as may further dispose them to a more comfortable communion with God in his public ordinances.

That all the people meet so timely for public worship that the whole congregation may be present at the beginning, and with one heart solemnly join together in all parts of the public worship, and not depart till after the blessing.

That what time is vacant, between or after the solemn meetings of the congregation in public, be spent in reading, meditation, repetition of services (especially by calling their families to an account of what they have heard, and catechising of them), holy conferences, prayer for a blessing upon the public ordinances, singing of Psalms, visiting the sick, relieving the poor, and such like duties of piety, charity, and mercy, accounting the Sabbath a delight."

Earnest attempts were made to improve the morals of the people, but the zeal of the Puritans was often not tempered with mercy, and frequently displayed a want of common-sense. In America, the Puritans made some very curious Sunday laws. Walking, riding, cooking, and many other natural needs of life were forbidden. Sports and recreations were punished by a fine of forty shillings and a public whipping. In New England, a mother might not kiss her child on a Sunday. An English author, visiting America in the year 1699, supplies interesting details anent Sunday laws at that time. Says the traveller : " If you kiss a woman in public, though offered as a courteous salutation, if any information is given to the select members, both shall be whipped or fined." As a slight compensation for the severity of the regulation, he adds that the " good humoured lasses, to make amends, will kiss the offender in a corner." He adverts to the captain of a ship, who, on his return from a long voyage, met his wife in the street, and kissed her, and for the offence had to pay ten shillings. Another Boston man was fined the same amount for kissing his wife in his own garden. The culprit refused to pay the money and had to endure twenty lashes.

Tobacco, in Virginia, took the place of money as a medium of exchange. A person absenting himself from church was fined one pound of tobacco, and for slandering a clergyman, eight hundred pounds. Ten pounds covered the cost of a dinner, and eight pounds a gallon of strong ale, and innkeepers were forbidden to charge more.

An important Act was passed in the reign of Charles II., in the year 1676, for the better observance of the Lord's day. It prohibited travelling, the pursuit of business, and all sales, except that of milk. Old church records and other documents contain numerous references to Sunday travelling, and, as an example, we may state that it appears, from the books of St. James's Church, Bristol, at a vestry meeting, held in 1679, four persons were found guilty of walking "on foot to Bath on Lord's day," and were each fined twenty shillings.

In past ages, attending church was not a matter of choice, but one of obligation. Several Acts of Parliament were made bearing on this subject. Laws of Edward VI. and of Elizabeth provided

as follows : "That every inhabitant of the realm
or dominion shall diligently and faithfully, having
no lawful or reasonable excuse to be absent,
endeavour themselves to their parish church or
chapel accustomed ; or, upon reasonable let, to
some usual place where common prayer shall be
used—on Sundays and holy days—upon penalty of
forfeiting, for every non-attendance, twelve pence,
to be levied by the Churchwardens to the use of
the poor." The enactments regarding holy days
were allowed to be disregarded. In the
reign of James I., the penalty of a shilling
for not attending church on Sunday was
re-enforced. Sunday, only in respect of the
attendance at church, is named in the statutes of
William and Mary and George III., by which
exceptions in favour of dissenters from the
Church of England were made. Not a few suits
were commenced against persons for not attending church. An early case is noted in the church
book of St. James's, Bristol. On July 6th, 1598,
Henry Anstey, a resident in that parish, had, in
answer to a summons, to appear before the vestry
for not attending the church. At Kingston-on-
Thames, we gather from the parish accounts that
the local authorities, in 1635, " Received from idle

persons, being from the church on Sabbaths,
3s. 1od." Some more recent cases are named by
Professor Amos, in his Treatise on Sir Matthew
Hale's "History of the Pleas of the Crown." In
the year 1817, it is stated that, "at the Spring
Assizes of Bedford, Sir Montague Burgoyne was
prosecuted for having been absent from church
for several months; when the case was defeated
by proof of the defendant being indisposed. And
in the Report of the Prison Inspectors to the
House of Lords, in 1841, it appeared that, in
1830, ten persons were in prison for recusancy in
not attending their parish churches. A mother
was prosecuted by her own son. It is clear that,
in many instances, personal and not religious
feeling gave rise to the actions." The laws
respecting recusants were repealed in the year
1844.

## The Easter Sepulchre.

SEVERAL of our old churches contain curious stone structures called Easter Sepulchres. They are generally on the north side of the chancel, and resemble, in design, a tomb. Before the Reformation, it was the practice on the evening of Good Friday, to place the Crucifix and Host in these sepulchres with much ceremony. Numerous candles were lighted, and watchers stood by until the dawn of Easter Day. Then, with every sign of devotion, the Crucifix and Host were once more removed to the altar, and the church re-echoed with joyous praise.

Concerning this ceremony, Cranmer says that it was done "In remembrance of Christ's sepulture, which was prophesied by Esaias to be glorious, and to signify there was buried the pure and undefiled body of Christ, without spot of sin, which was never separated from the Godhead, and, therefore, as David expressed it in the fifteenth Psalm, it could not see corruption, nor death detain or hold Him, but, He should rise again, to our great hope and comfort; and, therefore, the church adorns it with lights to express the great joy they have of that glorious triumph over death, the devil, and hell."

We have adverted to Easter Sepulchres of stone remaining at the present time, but they were by no means the only description erected. The Rev. Mackenzie E. C. Walcott, in his " Sacred Archæology," names, as follow, five sorts of sepulchres. The first, a chapel, as at Winchester; second, a wall recess, usually in the north side of the chancel, as at Bottesford, Lincolnshire, and Stanton St. John; third, a temporary structure, sumptuously enriched, as at St. Mary, Redcliffe, Bristol; fourth, a tomb, under which a founder, by special privilege, was buried; fifth, a vaulted enclosure, as at Norwich, which, like a sepulchre at Northwold, has an aperture for watching the light, without requiring the person so employed to enter the choir.

There was an imposing example at Seville, raised over the tomb of Columbus. It was constructed of wood, and was three storeys high, and brilliantly lighted. According to an old poet :

"With tapers all the people come, and at the barriars stay,
  Where downe upon their knees they fall, and night and
      day they pray,
  And violets and every kinde of flowers about the grave
  They straw, and bring all their giftes and presents that
      they have."

We are told that in many places, the steps of the sepulchre were covered with black cloth. Soldiers in armour, keeping guard, rendered the ceremony impressive. A gentleman named Roger Martin, who lived at the time of the Reformation, wrote an interesting account of the church of Melford, Suffolk. The following particulars are drawn from his manuscript respecting the Easter Sepulchre : " In the quire, there was a fair painted frame of timber, to be set up about Maunday Thursday, with holes for a number of fair tapers to stand in before the sepulchre, and to be lighted in the service time. Sometimes, it was set overthwart the quire, before the high altar, the sepulchre being alwaies placed, and finely garnished, at the north end of high altar, between that and Mr. Clopton's little chapel there, in a vacant place of the wall, I think upon a tomb

I

of one of his ancestors, the said frame with the
tapers was set near to the steps going up to the
said altar." The tomb referred to is that of John
Clopton, Esquire, of Kentwell Hall, who filled
the office of Sheriff of the county of Suffolk in
the year 1451, and died in 1497. An inventory
of church goods belonging to Melford Church,
under date of April 6th, 1541, has a statement to
the effect that " There was given to the church of
Melford, two stained cloths, whereof the one
hangeth towards Mr. Martin's ile, and the other
to be used about the sepulchre at Easter time."

In a curious work entitled " The Ancient Rites
and Monuments of the Monastical and Cathedral
Church of Durham," collected from out of ancient
manuscripts about the time of the suppression,
and published by J. D. (Davies), of Kidwelly, in
1672, there is an interesting account of a custom
enacted at Durham. The following account is
supposed to have been written in 1593, and, perhaps, by one who took part in the ceremonies, at
all events, the writer was conversant with them.
" Within the Church of Durham, upon Good
Friday, there was a marvellous solemn service,
in which service time, after the Passion was sung,
two of the ancient monks took a goodly large

crucifix, all of gold, of the picture of our Saviour
Christ, nayled upon the cross. . . . The service
being ended, the said two monks carried the cross
to the sepulchre with great reverence, which
sepulchre was set up in the morning on the north
side of the quire, nigh the high altar, before the
service time, and they did lay it within the said
sepulchre with great devotion, with another
picture of our Saviour Christ, in whose Breast
they did enclose, with great reverence, the most
holy and blessed Sacrament of the Altar, censing
and praying unto it upon their knees, a great
space ; and setting two lighted tapers before it,
which did burn till Easter Day in the morning,
at which time it was taken forth. . . . There was
very solemn service betwixt three and four
of the clock in the morning, in honour of the
Resurrection, where two of the eldest monks in
the quire came to the sepulchre, set up upon
Good Fryday, after the Passion, all covered with
red velvet embroider'd with gold, and did then
cense it, either of the monks with a pair of silver
censers, sitting on their knees before the sepulchre.
Then they, both rising, came to the sepulchre,
out of which, with great reverence, they took a
marvellous beautiful image of our Saviour, repre-

senting the Resurrection, with a cross in his hand,
on the breast was enclosed, in most bright
chrystal, the holy Sacrament of the Altar,
through which chrystal, the Blessed Host was
conspicious to the beholders. Then, after the
elevation of the said picture, carried by the said
two monks, upon a fair velvet cushion, all
embroider'd, singing the anthems of *Christus
Resurgens*, they brought it to the high altar." We
gather from the preceding and other accounts,
that the sepulchre at Durham was a temporary
erection, consisting of a wooden framework,
having silk hangings.

As might be expected, much interesting
information may be found in old churchwardens'
accounts bearing on this theme. The records of
St. Mary Redcliffe Church, Bristol, contain the
following entries :

" Item—That Maister Canynge hath delivered,
this 4th day of July, in the year of Our Lord
1470, to Maister Nicholas Petters, vicar of St.
Mary Redcliffe, Moses Conterin, Philip
Bartholomew, Procurators of St. Mary Redcliffe
aforesaid, a new sepulchre, well gilt with golde,
and a civer thereto.

Item—An image of God Almighty rising out

of the same sepulchre, with all the ordinance that longeth thereto ; that is to say, a lathe made of timber, and the ironwork thereto.

Item—Thereto longeth Heaven, made of timber and stayned clothes.

EASTER SEPULCHRE AT PATRINGTON.

Item—Hell, made of timber, and the ironwork thereto, with Divels to the number of 13.

Item—4 Knights, armed, keeping the sepulchre, with their weapons in their hands ; that is to say,

2 axes and 2 spears, with 2 paves.   [A pave was a shield.]

Item—4 payr of Angels wings for 4 Angels, made of timber, and well painted.

Item—The Fadre [*i.e.*, the Father], the Crowne and Visage, the ball with a cross upon it, well gilt with fine gould.

Item—The Holy Ghost coming out of Heaven into the sepulchre.

Item—Longeth to the 4 Angels 4 Chevelures."

We cull from the accounts of St. Helen's, Abingdon, Berkshire, some quaint items as follows :

> " 1557.   To the sexton for watching the sepulter two nights, 8d.
>
> 1559.   Payde for making the sepulture, 10s.
>
> For peynting the same sepulture, 3s.
>
> For stones and other charges about it, 4s. 6d.
>
> To the sexten, for meat and drink and watching the sepulture according to custom, 22d."

In this case, of course, the sepulchre was merely a temporary erection.   In the church-wardens' accounts of Waltham Abbey Church are the following entries :

" 1542.	Payde for watching the sepulchre, 4d.

1544.	Payde for watching the sepulchre, 8d. "

Amongst the churches of this country where permanent Easter Sepulchres still remain, are the following : Heckington, Navenby, Northwold, Holcombe, Burnell, Southpool, Hawton, and Patrington. We give an illustration of the interesting example at Patrington, East Yorkshire. Mr. Bloxham speaks of it as probably the work of the earlier years of the fifteenth century. The carvings are of freestone, and represent the watching of three soldiers, beneath three ogee-shaped canopies. On their shields are heraldic designs. The other figures represent our Saviour, emerging from the tomb, and two angels are raising the lid of the coffin. This is certainly a very interesting example, but perhaps not so fine as those of Navenby and Heckington, Lincolnshire.

## St. Paul's Cross.

EATH on the cross was regarded as the most degrading form of capital punishment. The Romans executed on it only slaves and the lowest class of malefactors. It was a cruel mode of punishment, as a person might linger alive on it for days. It was customary to erect crosses without the gates of towns, but in places largely frequented by the people. The name of the criminal, and the nature of his offence, were inscribed on a tablet, for the information of the public. The crucifixion of Christ on the cross, has caused Christians to reverence it, and the sign of the cross to be regarded as a holy sign.

In bygone times, crosses of various kinds might be seen in England in every direction. A writer says that they were as common in the olden days as milestones are at the present time.

The Island of Iona, it is asserted, once possessed
360 crosses, but now only one is left, the
famous runic cross of St. Martin's. Some interesting examples of runic crosses still remain, and a
good specimen may still be seen in the church-

EYAM CROSS.

yard of Eyam, Derbyshire. It is generally
supposed to have been brought to the churchyard
from the adjacent moor. The cross is richly
embellished with symbolical devices on the arms,
some figures are blowing trumpets, others holding

crosses, and one holding a book.  On one side
of the shaft is a carving of the Virgin and Child.

A complete history of the cross cannot be
attempted here.  We must, in this chapter, content
ourselves with an account of the Preaching Cross
of St. Paul's, London.  Its history is linked with
the religious and political life of England.
Preaching crosses were by no means uncommon
in bygone times, and the most famous was the
one under notice.  It is not known when a pulpit
cross was first erected at St. Paul's, but it has
been ascertained that it was standing in 1241,
and that most likely it existed long prior to that
period.

The Mayor, in 1259, was commanded by
Henry III., to compel all city youths who had
reached the age of fourteen and upwards, to take,
at St. Paul's Cross, an oath of allegiance to him
and his heirs.

In 1382, the cross was thrown down by an earthquake.  An effort was soon made by the Bishop
of London to rebuild the cross, and indulgences
were granted to those who contributed to the work.
The Rev. W. Sparrow Simpson, D.D., F.S.A., in his
"Chapters in the History of Old St. Paul's,"
gives the following literal translation of the

original document, which is still preserved in the Cathedral record-room: "To the sons of our Holy Mother, the Church, under whose notice, these present letters shall come, William, by Divine permission, Archbishop of Canterbury, Primate of all England, and Legate of the Apostolic See, wishes eternal health in the Lord. We esteem it a service pleasant and acceptable to God, whensoever, by the alluring gifts of indulgences, we stir up the minds of the faithful to a greater readiness in contributing their gifts to such works as concern the honour of the Divine Name. Since then, the High Cross in the greater church-yard of the Church of London (where the Word of God is habitually preached both to the clergy and laity, being a place very public and well known), by strong winds and tempests of the air and terrible earthquakes, hath become so frail and injured, that, unless some means be quickly taken for its repair and restoration, it will fall utterly into ruin ; therefore, by the mercy of Almighty God, trusting in the merits and prayers of the most Blessed Virgin Mary, His Mother, and of the Blessed Apostles, Peter and Paul, and of all the Saints, We, by these presents, mercifully grant in the Lord, to all the servants of Christ through-

out our province of Canterbury, wheresoever
living, truly repenting and confessing their sins,
who, for the restoration and repair of the aforesaid
Cross, shall give, bequeath, or in any manner
assign, of the goods committed to them, gifts of
charity, Forty Days of Indulgence.  In testimony
whereof, we have to this present letter affixed our
seal.  Given in Manor of Fulham, in the diocese
of London, on the 18th May, in the year of our
Lord one thousand, three hundred, and eighty-
seven, and in the sixth year of our translation."

This document was not confined to London
and its neighbourhood, the Bishops of Ely, Bath,
Chester, Carlisle, Llandaff, and Bangor approved
of it, and assisted in its circulation in their
dioceses.  Bishop Kempe, who held the see of
London, appears to have been active in this
movement.  The amount realised by means of
the indulgences is not known, but sufficient was
collected to enable the Bishop of London to
rebuild the cross.

Penitents, under ecclesiastical censure, came
here to perform public penance; and perhaps
the most familiar name of those who came is
Jane Shore.  It was in the year 1483 that she
did public penance.  She was one of the

mistresses of Edward IV., who died in 1483,
and, within two months of his death, she was tried
by Richard III. for sorcery and witchcraft, but he
failed in proving his charges. He took property
from her equal to about £20,000 of the present
time. His next step was to bring her before the
Ecclesiastical Courts and have her tried for
incontinence. It was for this crime that she had
to do penance in the streets of London. She
proceeded from the Bishop's Palace, clothed in a
white sheet, and carrying in her hand a wax taper,
and before her was carried a cross. We are told
by Rowe:

> " Submissive, sad, and lowly was her look,
> A burning taper in her hand she bore,
> And on her shoulders, carelessly confus'd
> With loose neglect, her lovely tresses hung,
> Upon her cheeks a faintish flush was spread,
> Feeble she seem'd, and sorely smit with pain,
> While barefoot as she trod the flinty pavement,
> Her footsteps all along were mark'd with blood.
> Yet silent still she pass'd, and unrepining,
> Her streaming eyes bent ever on the earth,
> Except when, in some bitter pang of sorrow,
> To Heaven she seem'd in fervent zeal to raise
> And beg that mercy man denied her here."

It was on June 19th, 1483, that Dr. Ralph
Shaw, brother of the Lord Mayor, preached a

famous sermon at the cross.   Richard, Duke of
Gloucester, intended seizing the crown.   Dr.
Shaw was directed to make the purpose known in
his sermon, and, accordingly, took for his text the
fourth chapter of the Book of Wisdom : " Bastard
slips shall not take root."   He tried to prove the
illegitimacy of Edward V. and his brother, saying
that when Edward IV. married their mother,
Elizabeth Woodville, he was already the husband
of Lady Eleanor Boteler, of Sudeley.   Next, he
expressed a doubt if Edward was in reality the
son of Richard, Duke of York, and entitled
to the crown of England.   He made a strong
point of the fact that no likeness existed between
him and his reputed father.   Continuing his sermon,
he observed that " my Lord Protector, that very
noble prince, the pattern of all heroic deeds,
represented the very face and mind of the great
Duke, his father ; he is the perfect image of his
father ; his features are the same, and the very
express likeness of that noble Duke."   Sir
Thomas More says that it had been arranged
that, when the words had been spoken, the
Protector should have come amongst the assembly,
" to the end that these words, reciting with his
presence, might have been taken by the hearers

as though the Holy Ghost had put them in the
preacher's mouth, and should have moved the
people even then to cry, ' King Richard! King
Richard!' that it might have been after said that
he was specially chosen by God, and in a manner
by miracle. But the device failed, either by the
Protector's negligence, or the preacher's over-
much diligence." There is not any evidence that
the device was contemplated. It is suggested
that the sermon is not correctly reported, and it is
believed that Richard would not have submitted
to any aspersion on the chastity of his mother.

William Tyndale's translation of the Bible was
publicly burned in front of the cross in the year
1527. "Cardinal Wolsey," writes W. H.
Davenport Adams, in his " Book about London,"
"sat enthroned in the midst of bishops, mitred
abbots, and princes, and attended by a large
concourse of chaplains and spiritual doctors.
Opposite, on a platform, knelt six heretics, clothed
in penitential garb—one holding a lighted taper
of five pounds weight, the others carrying
symbolic faggots, signifying the fate they had
deserved, though, this time, mercifully allowed to
escape it. After they had made confession of
their errors, and begged pardon of God and the

Holy Catholic Church, Bishop Fisher preached a sermon. The penitents were then conducted to a great fire which had been kindled in front of the north door of the cathedral, and led round it thrice, casting in their faggots as they went." The ceremony concluded by Testaments and tracts being cast into the blazing fire.

Shortly after Mary had occupied the throne, a serious riot occurred at the cross. On Sunday, August 13th, 1553, Bourne, the Queen's chaplain, preached to a large gathering of refugees and English fanatics. In the course of his sermon, he prayed for the souls of the departed, praised Bonner, and spoke in an uncharitable manner of Ridley. He was assailed with cries of " Papist, Papist! Tear him down!" A dagger was thrown at him, but, striking one of the side-posts of the cross, missed him. Men drew their swords, and had not leading Protestants interfered, doubtless Bourne would have lost his life, and those who supported him would have suffered. Fox, in his "Acts and Monuments," relates how Master Bradford came into the pulpit, and "spoke so mildly, christianly, and effectously that, with few words, he appeased all : and afterward he and Master Rogers conducted the preacher betwixt them from the pulpit to the grammar school door, where they left him safe." Shortly afterwards, the two men who had intervened were cast into prison, and finally suffered death at the fires of Smithfield.

Determined efforts were made to proclaim the doctrines of the Roman Catholic Church, and on the following Sunday, Mr. Thomas Watson, an earnest preacher, gave a stirring sermon. He was guarded with 200 soldiers, "with their halberdes." Amongst those who listened to him, are named the Marquis of Winchester, the Earl of Bedford, the Earl of Pembroke, and the Lord Rich. Watson, some time previously, had been set in the stocks at Canterbury, by the orders of Cranmer. The time was near at hand when the teachings of the Roman Church were "heard without protest, if not with approval." The Catholics took decided measures to close the mouths of those who did not agree with them.

Mary died. In her stead, Elizabeth occupied the throne, and a change came over the scene. The new Queen dearly loved pomp. On one occasion, she went to hear one of the Reformers preach at St. Paul's, and in her train were a large number of lords and ladies, 1000 soldiers, ten

K

great cannons, hundreds of drums and trumpets, a party of morris-dancers, and two white bears. On Ash Wednesday, 1565, Dean Nowell preached. Queen Elizabeth was present, and a very large number of the inhabitants of London, doubtless being more anxious to see their Queen than listen to the preacher. The Dean had not proceeded far with his sermon when he came to the subject of images, which, we are told, " he handled roughly." The Queen cried out : " Leave them alone." He did not hear her, and continued his invectives. Raising her voice, she said : " To your text, Mr. Dean ! to your text ! Leave that, we have heard enough of that ! To your subject !" The Dean stammered a few more incoherent words, and was obliged to give up any further attempts to continue his sermon. The Queen left the place in a rage, and the Protestant part of the congregation, we are told, were moved to tears.

The most able preachers of the day, including Latimer, Cranmer, and other great men, delivered sermons at St. Paul's Cross, and it was recognised as the seat of pulpit eloquence. Sermons were lightly esteemed unless preached here. The preachers were lodged at the

Shunamite House for two days before and for one day after their sermon, and suitable diet provided for them. Soon after Richard Hooker had taken his degree (1581), he was invited to preach at the cross. He arrived in London wet and weary, and ill with a severe cold. He was carefully tended and cured by Mrs. Churchman, who had charge of the Shunamite House. Her consideration did not end with her nursing. She persuaded Hooker that he was "a man of tender constitution," and that it would be his wisest course to have a wife who would nurse him. Not only would a wife prolong his life, but would make him more comfortable. Mrs. Churchman suggested her own daughter as a desirable wife. Hooker had not courage to refuse the proposal, and in due course they were married. The union was in every respect unsuitable. She is described as being without beauty and portion, and, worse still, she was of a shrewish temper.

The Dean of St. Paul's, in 1588, gave public notice at the cross of the defeat of the "Invincible Armada." Important local, as well as national, events were made known here. It was here and in similar places, says a recent writer, "Londoners must have first heard of the triumphs at Cressy and Poictiers—of their glorious Black Prince and his captive, King John ; as in a latter age of the victory at Agincourt." Public announcements in past ages were very important when few could read.

We read, in an old record, that on the birthday of Queen Elizabeth, on the 17th November, 1595, "the Pulpit Cross, in St. Paul's Church-yard, was new repaired, painted, and partly enclosed with a wall of brick. Doctor Fletcher, Bishop of London, preached there in praise of the Queen, and prayed for her Majesty, before the Lord Mayor, Aldermen, and Citizens, in their best liveries. Which sermon being ended, upon the church-leades the trumpets sounded, the cornets winded, and the quiristers sung an antheme. On the steeple many lights were burned, the Tower shot off her ordnance, the bels were rung, bone-fires made, etc."

The next event we notice at the cross, is in the reign of the first king of the ill-fated house of Stuart. For some years Henry Farley had, with pen and picture, done much to rouse an interest in St. Paul's Cathedral, which, for over half a century, had been in a dilapidated condition, the chief cause being the result of a fire in 1561.

In addition to trying to get bills introduced into Parliament, publishing pamphlets, he had, in 1616, pictures painted. One painting represented a procession of great personages; another, the said personages seated at a sermon at St. Paul's Cross. We reproduce a picture of his painting of the cross. In the gallery, placed against the choir of the church, are seated the King, Queen, Prince of Wales, the Lord Mayor, and other notable men and women, and a large gathering of citizens is seated in front of the cross. The dog-whipper is busy driving away a dog. The outcome of Farley's zeal, was the visit of James I., with his family and court, to hear a sermon here, on Midlent Sunday, in 1620. The gathering would be similar to the one represented in the picture drawn four years previously. The preacher was Dr. John King, called by James "The King of Preachers." He selected for his text, Psalm cii. 13, 14. "Thou wilt arise, and have mercy upon Zion; for the appointed time is come; for Thy servants delight in the stones thereof, and have pity on the dust thereof." It will, perhaps, not be without interest to give a few quotations from Dr. King's sermon, as a specimen of the extravagant figures of speech which prevailed at this period, and came down to the days of William III. "I am now," said Dr. King, "to speak unto you of litterall and artificial Zion

THE PREACHING CROSS, ST. PAUL'S.

—a temple without life, yet of a sicklie and crazie constitution, sicke of age itselfe, and with many aches in her joynts, together with a lingering consumption that hath long been in her bowels,

the timber in the beames whereof cryeth, ' I
perish,' and the stone on the walles answereth no
less, and part is already moultered away to stone,
part to dust, and (that which is more), symbolizing
with the other Zion, not only when fates and
casualties, but in the very retinues and revolu-
tions of these fates. After her building (600
years after Christ), salted with fire, sacrificed to
the anger of God, and being raised, Phœnix, out
of the ashes, betwixt 400 and 500 more (two in a
thousand years), touched by an invisible hand,
with a coal from the altar of heaven, that was
never blowne, which wholly consumed the crest
and vertical point, the top and top-gallant, and so
scorched the rest, that ever since it hath remained
valetudinary and infirm, rather peced out with an
ordinary kind of physic, than restored to a sound
plight." In conclusion, he said, " Set it as seale
upon your hearts, that your king has come unto
you. Such comings are not often ; Queen
Elizabeth once, and now your sovereign once.
Would it be believed, that a king should come
from his court to this cross, where princes seldom
or never come, and that ceremony to be in state,
with a kinde of sacred pompe and procession,
accompanied with all the fair flowers of his field,

and the fairest rose of his garden, to make requests to his subjects, not for his private, but for the public ; not for himselfe, but for God ; not out of reason, state policy, but of religion and piety ; no lesse fruit of honour and favour with God and man accruing thereby to his people, than to his sacred Majesty. You see it, value and prize it." James I. and others gave liberal donations towards the restoration fund, but it was not until the reign of Charles I. that any real progress was made. The king and Archbishop Laud were most active in carrying out the much-required work.

The story of St. Paul's Cross, and the interest that gathers round it, must here close. The Civil War is about to cast a gloom over the land, and bring misery to gentle and simple. The exact year the cross was pulled down is a disputed point, but most likely about 1643.

Carlyle, in his "Letters and Speeches of Cromwell," has the following striking passage : "Paul's Cross was a kind of stone tent, with leaden roof, at the N.E. corner of Paul's Cathedral, where sermons were still, and had long been, preached in the open air ; crowded devout congregations gathering there, with forms to sit on, if you came early. Queen Elizabeth used to 'tune her pulpits,' she said, when there was any great thing on hand ; as Governing Persons now strive to tune the Morning Newspapers. Paul's Cross, a kind of *Times Newspaper*, but edited partly by Heaven itself, was then a most important entity."

## Cheapside Cross.

AMONG the memorial crosses of Europe, those of Queen Eleanor are the most elegant and historically interesting. Edward I. was blessed with a devoted wife, who accompanied him in his expeditions and wars. He took part in the last of the Crusades, and was, by an assassin, wounded by a poisoned dagger. His wife, it is said, saved his life by sucking the venom from the wound. The English people greatly loved her; she was ever ready to comfort those in trouble, and redress wrongs. She was married in 1254, in her fifteenth year, and died at Harby or Hardeby, Nottinghamshire, on November 20th, 1290, when on her way to join the king in Scotland. She appears to have been ill for some time, and, on October 18th, six weeks before her death, a mark (13s. 4d.) was paid to Henry of Montpellier for syrups and other medicines for the queen's use. Leopardo, her own physician, was in attendance. The king deeply mourned her loss, and had her remains conveyed to Westminster Abbey for interment. An elegant cross was erected at every place where the funeral procession rested. Fifteen of these crosses have been traced. The details of the queen's death and burial are hotly-contested historical problems, and no two historians agree in their statements. Of the crosses erected by Edward, only three remain, those at Northampton, Gedington, and Waltham Cross. A picture of the Northampton Cross, as it appears to-day, enables us to realise how elegant it must have been when newly erected, and before time's defacing touch and man's mischief had robbed it of much of its beauty.

The idea of the Eleanor Crosses was not a new one, it was, as is stated by Rimmer, in his "Ancient Stone Crosses of England," "an extension of the lich-gate system, for a corpse always rested under a 'lich.'" At the churchyard gates in some places, notably in Cornwall, are large lich-stones, on which to rest the coffin while the funeral procession is waiting for the officiating minister. At St. Winnow, Cornwall, an example

may be seen.   In some parts of the country, as at
Lustleigh, Devonshire, there are resting stones
for the coffin on its way to the burial ground,
some distance from the church.   The coverings
over the lich-gates are usually of wood, but sometimes they are of stone, as at Birstal, near Leeds.
At Barking, Essex, are chambers over the lich-
gate, and one was formerly known as the Chapel
of the Holy Rood.   In other parts of the country
are examples of chambers over the lich-gate.   A
great many of the kings of France were buried at
the Abbey of St. Denis, and on the road leading to
it from Paris, crosses were erected at almost every
few hundred yards.   The Revolution swept away
the monuments.

The cross at Cheape was an Eleanor Cross,
and erected shortly after the death of the queen.
It is generally believed that this cross was one of
the finest of its class, but no reliable description
has come down to us.   Master Michael, a mason
of Canterbury, was its builder.

In 1441, the rebuilding of this cross, in
combination with a drinking fountain, was
commenced, and was hardly completed in 1486.
Timber and lead were largely used in the second
erection, which was frequently regilded.   It

NORTHAMPTON CROSS.

appears to have attained its greatest beauty in the
reign of Edward VI.    At his accession to the
throne, it underwent considerable alterations and
improvements.

A painting of the period, shewing the procession
of Edward VI. to his Coronation, gives us a good
idea of the cross as it appeared in 1547.    It may
be briefly described as stately and graceful.
There are three octangular compartments, and
each is supported by eight slender columns.    Its
height is calculated at about thirty-six feet; the
first storey being about twenty feet, the second,
ten, and the third, six.    Amongst the statues
which ornamented the structure may be mentioned, in the first niche, most likely, a con-
temporaneous pope, round the base of the second
were four apostles, and above them was placed
the Virgin, with the infant Jesus in her arms.
Four standing figures filled the top niche, and a
cross, surmounted with the emblematic dove,
completed the ornamentation, which was extremely
rich.

It long remained a pride of the city, but as
time ran its course changes of sentiment came
about.    Towards the close of Elizabeth's reign, it
was denounced as a relic of Popish superstition.

On the night of the 21st June, 1581, an attack was made by some fanatics on the monument, and much of the carving mutilated. "The Virgin," says an old writer, "was robbed of her son, and her arms broken, by which she staid him on her knees; her whole body was haled by ropes, and left ready to fall." Although a reward was offered by the queen, the offenders were not discovered. Fourteen years later, the effigy of the Virgin was repaired, and "a newe sonne, misshapen (as borne out of time), all naked, was laide in her armes, the other images continuing broken as before."

Next, an attempt was made to remove the woodwork, and in place of the crucifix erect a pyramid. A figure of the goddess Diana replaced the Virgin. Diana was represented for the most part naked, "and water, conveyed from the Thames, filtering through her naked breasts, but oftentimes dryed up." Elizabeth expressed her displeasure at the operations of the fanatics, and gave directions for a plain gilt cross to be placed on the summit of the monument, saying such a simple symbol of the faith of the country ought not to cause scandal. The Virgin was again restored, but, in less than a fortnight, the figure was mutilated, and the child taken away.

In 1600, the cross was rebuilt, and the question of restoring the crucifix gave rise to considerable discussion. The matter was referred to the authorities of the Universities. All sanctioned it except Dr. Abbot, afterwards Archbishop of Canterbury, but there was not to be a dove. In a sermon of the period, the following passage occurs : " Oh ! this cross is one of the jewels of the harlot of Rome, and is left and kept here as a love-token, and gives them hope that they shall enjoy it and us again." The new cross, which was protected by strong iron railings, was much inferior to the preceding one. In style, it was half Grecian and half Gothic. Images of a superstitious character were superseded by those of apostles, kings, and, prelates, and of the original cross only the crucifix was retained. For many years, it remained without giving rise to any contention. The Puritanical zeal increased in course of time, and on the night of January 24th, 1641, it again suffered at the hands of the fanatics.

At this time, commenced a literary warfare, in the form of pamphlets, respecting the cross. These were followed by its destruction. Robert Harlow was deputed by Parliament to carry out the work. He went to the cross with a troop of horse and two companies of foot soldiers. How completely he executed his orders may be gathered from the official account. It states : "On the 2nd of May, 1643, the cross in Cheapside was pulled down. At the fall of the top cross, drums

PURITANS DESTROYING CHEAPSIDE CROSS.

beat, trumpets blew, and multitudes of caps were thrown in the air, and a great shout of people with joy. The 2nd of May, the almanack says, was the invention of the cross, and the same day, at night, were the leaden popes burnt [they were not popes, but eminent English prelates] in the place

L

where it stood, with ringing of bells and a great acclamation, and no hurt at all done in these actions."

The author of "The Old City" (London, 1865), a work to which we have been indebted for some of the particulars included in this paper, adverts to a curious tract published on the day the cross was destroyed. It bears the following title: "The Downfall of Dagon; or, the taking down of Cheapside Crosse; wherein is contained these principalls: 1. The crosse sicke at heart. 2. His death and funerall. 3. His will, legacies, inventory, and epitaph. 4. Why it was removed. 5. The money it will bring. 6. Noteworthy, that it was cast down on that day when it was first invented and set up." An extract or two from this publication can hardly fail to interest the reader. "I am called the 'Citie Idoll,'" says the tract, "the Brownists spit at me, and throw stones at me; the Famalists hide their eyes with their fingers; the Anabaptists wish me knockt in pieces, as I am to be this day; the sisters of the fraternity will not come near me, but go by Watling Street, and come in again by Soaper Lane, to buy provisions of the market folks. . . . I feele the pangs of death, and shall never see the end of the merry month of May; my breath stops—my life is gone; I feel myself a-dying downards." The bequests embrace the following: "I give my iron work to those which make good swords at Hounslow, for I am Spanish iron and steele to the backe. I give my body and stones to those masons that cannot telle how to frame the like againe, to keep by theme for a patterne, for in time there will be more crosses in London than ever there was yet." The epitaph is as follows:

> "I looke for no praise when I am dead,
> For, going the right way, I never did tread.
> I was harde as an Alderman's doore,
> That's shut and stony-hearted to the poore.
> I never gave almes, nor did anything
> Was good, nor e'er said, 'God save the King.'
> I stood like a stock that was made of wood,
> And yet the people would not say I was good,
> And, if I tell them plaine, they're like to mee—
> Like stone to all goodnesse. But now, reader, see
> Me in the dust; for crosses must not stand,
> There is too much crosse tricks within the land;
> And, having so done never any good,
> I leave my prayse for to be understood;
> For many women, after this my losse,
> Will remember me, and still will be crosse—
> Crosse tricks, crosse ways, and crosse vanities.
> Believe the crosse speaks truth, for here he lyes."

## The Biddenden Maids Charity.

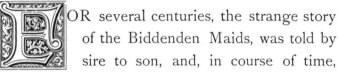

FOR several centuries, the strange story of the Biddenden Maids, was told by sire to son, and, in course of time, was made the subject of a broadside, which has become rare, and is much prized by collectors of historical curiosities.

The tale is to the effect that, in the year of our Lord, 1100, at the village of Biddenden, in the county of Kent, were born Eliza and Mary Chulkhurst, commonly called "The Biddenden Maids." It is asserted that the sisters were joined together by the hips and shoulders.

There is not a record of any attempt being made to separate the couple, and they grew up together. When they had attained the age of thirty-four years, one of the sisters was taken ill, and shortly afterwards died. The surviving one was entreated to submit to a surgical operation being performed, and have her body separated from that of her deceased sister, but she firmly refused. She was prepared to die. "As we came together," she said,

BIDDENDEN CAKE.

"we will also go together." Her life closed about six hours after that of her sister.

The claims of the poor were not overlooked. The sisters, in their will, bequeathed to the churchwardens of the parish of Biddenden, a piece of land which is known as " Bread and Cheese Land."

The rent of it realises a considerable sum of money, which is largely distributed to the poor of the place in bread and cheese.

The memory of the wonderful women is maintained by the distribution, on Easter Sunday, of about a thousand small cakes made of flour and water, and having impressed upon them rude representations of the Maids.

Hone, in his " Every Day Book," gives a picture of the cake he received in 1826, which we reproduce. It is the exact size of the one sent to him. Since Hone's time a new stamp or mould has been made, and the old style of representing the Maids has not been followed in every detail. In the cut we give, it will be noticed no legs appear, now they are represented on the cakes.

In addition to the small cakes presented to strangers as well as villagers, every resident in the parish is entitled to a threepenny loaf and three quarters of a pound of cheese. The charity was formerly delivered at the tower door of the church, but since some alterations have been made in the building, the distribution takes place at the old workhouse. The congregation, on Easter Sunday afternoon, after which service the cakes are given, is always very large, many persons coming from the surrounding villages.

Halsted, the historian of Kent, discredits the traditional origin of the old custom. A similiar story is related of two females, whose figures appear on the pavement of Norton St. Philip's Church, Somersetshire.

## Plagues and Pestilences.

THE graphic pages of Daniel Defoe have made the reader familiar with the terrible story of the Great Plague of London, which began in December, 1664, and carried off 68,596 persons, some say even a larger number. To give a detailed account of that visitation would be to relate an oft-told tale. Some important facts, not generally known, respecting old-time plagues and pestilences may be gleaned from parish registers and church-wardens' accounts, and it is from such records that we propose mainly to draw materials for this chapter.

When a town was infected with the plague, business was suspended, and the inhabitants isolated from the neighbouring places. If a person desired to travel at large, he made appli-cation to the Mayor or Chief Magistrate, and obtained a certificate to the effect that he was not suspected of the plague.

In many towns, great wisdom was displayed by erecting huts on breezy moors and other places away from the busy haunts of men, for the reception of the plague-stricken persons, and to which they were removed. The inmates of a house were not suffered to leave the homes from whence the patients had been removed. An order passed in London, in 1570, states: "Howses, having some sicke, though none die, or from whence some sicke have been removed, are infected houses, and such are to be shutt upp for a moneth. The whole family to tarrie xxviii daies." Round the houses, watch and ward were constantly kept to prevent egress. Certain boundaries were defined, and these could not be passed. The watchers provided the inmates of the houses with food, etc., and took messages to their friends. In the churchwardens' accounts of St. Mary, Woolchurch, Haw, is an entry :—

" 1607-8.   Paid a warder for warding

Mr. Clarke's house, being infected,

ordered by the Mayor .............. 4   0."

On the door of the infected house was the sign of a cross, in a flaming red colour, with the pathetic prayer, "Lord, have mercy on us." In old church-wardens' accounts, many items like the following, drawn from the accounts of St. Mary, Woolnoth, London, might be quoted :

> " 1593-4.   Item for setting a crosse
> upon one Allen's doore in the
> sicknesse time ....................... ijd.
>   Item paid for setting two red crosses
> upon Anthony Sound his dore... iiijd."

These crosses were about a foot in length. More than one student of the past has suggested that the practice of marking the doors of infected houses with red crosses arose from the injunction given to Moses at the institution of the passover. The crosses served the important purpose for which they were intended, namely, to caution folk against going to infected houses.

Queen Elizabeth, in 1563, commanded that the inmates of a house which had been visited by the plague should not go to church for a month.

Orders were given that any dogs found in the streets were to be killed. An order, bearing on this matter, made in May, 1583, at Winchester, may be reproduced: "That if any house wtn this cytie shall happen to be infected with the Plague, that thene evye persone to keepe within

his or her house every his or her dogg, and not
to suffer them to goo at large : And if any dogg
be then founde abroad at large, it shall be lawful
for the Beadle or any other person to kill the
same dogg : and that any Owner of such Dogg
going at large shall lose 6s." It was believed
that dogs conveyed contagion from infected
houses. A passage in Homer's " Iliad" has a
reference to man obtaining infection from an
animal. It relates to the great pestilence that
prevailed in the Grecian army :

> " On mules and beasts the infection first began,
> At last, its vengeful arrows fix'd in man ;
> Apollo's wrath the dire disorder spread,
> And heap'd the camp with mountains of the dead.
> For nine long nights throughout the dusky air,
> The funeral torches shed a dismal glare."

Many remedies were tried to stay the progress
of plagues. The ringing of church bells was
among the number. " Great ringing of bells in
populous cities," says Bacon, in his " Natural
History," " disperseth pestilent air, which may be
from the concussion of the air, and not from the
sound." Music, in the Middle Ages, was believed
to have a healing power. Large fires were lighted
in houses and streets as preventatives. It is not
unlikely that the practice may be derived from

the fact that, in 1347, during the time of the plague raging at Avignon, Pope Clement VI. caused great fires to be kept in his palace, day and night, and by this means believed he had kept the pestilence from his household. In 1563, we learn from Stow that a commandment came from Queen Elizabeth that "every man in every street and lane should make a bonefire three times a week, in order to the ceasing of the plague, if it so pleased God, and so to continue these fires everywhere, Mondays, Wednesdays, and Fridays."

It is asserted in Rome, in A.D. 195, that for some time, 5,000 persons died daily of a fearful plague. The physicians were unable to check its deadly course. It lasted for three years. The doctors of the day urged upon the people to fill their noses and ears with sweet smelling ointments to prevent contagion. We learn from Defoe's " Journal of the Plague Year, 1665," how largely perfumes, aromatics, and essences, were employed to escape contagion at that time. Says Defoe, if you went into a church where any number of people were present, " there would be such a mixture of smells at the entrance, that it was much more strong, though, perhaps, not so wholesome, than if you were going into an apothecary's or druggist's shop. In a word, the whole church was like a smelling bottle; in one corner, it was all perfumes; in another, aromatics, balsamics, and a variety of drugs and herbs; in another, salts and spirits; as every one was furnished for their own preservation." He further says : " The poorer people, who only set open their windows night and day, burnt brimstone, pitch, and gunpowder, and such things in their rooms, did as well as the best."

The annals of many of the northern English towns contain numerous sad references to plagues. Newcastle-upon-Tyne, for example, suffered much. The churchwardens' accounts of St. Nicholas contain records of payments which bear on this subject. We find, for instance, the following item :

" 1699.    By cash paid for a tarr barrell
        to burn in ye church .............. o    8."

Fires were made in churches in movable pans. A year later, we read :

" 1700.    For hearbs for rubing ye
        pewes ............................. 1    o."

In courts of justice, might be seen large nose-gays, not for ornament, but as preservatives against the pest.    The Rev. J. R. Boyle, F.S.A.,

has gone carefully over the churchwardens'
accounts of St. Nicholas', now the Cathedral of
the city of Newcastle, and reproduced some
curious items in his guide to the building. Here
follow a few of the items :

"1684.   For juniper and erbes for ye

vestry ................................. o  10.

1684.   Paid for erbes and fflowers

for Mr. Maior's pew 2 times ...... 3   0.

1686.   Erbes for ye church at Easter,

Whitsuntyde, and Assizes ......... 6   0.

1688.   Paid for holland [holly] and

juniper for ye vestery, and erbs ... 1  11.

1690.   Paid for sweet herbs for

strawing in ye pews, etc............. 1   0."

Mr. William Kelly, read before the Royal
Historical Society, on July 12th, 1877, an
important paper on "Visitations of the Plague at
Leicester." He gave particulars of the Mayor
addressing a letter to Justice Gawdie, who was
about to visit the town in his official capacity.
He was informed that the plague had broken out
in houses near the castle, and it was concluded
that his lordship would not come to preside so
near the infected places. The result of the
communication may be gathered from the follow-

ing entry, copied from the chamberlain's accounts :

"1594. Item, paid for charges of makinge readye of All Hallowes Churche for the judges to hold the assyses in, because the other parte of the town was then infected with the sicknes .................... xvs. vjd."

We have previously stated, that persons wishing to leave a plague-stricken town, for the purpose of travelling, were obliged to obtain passes. Mr. Kelly gives a copy of one of these documents, which we reproduce *in extenso*. It reads as follows :

"Villa Leic. Theise are to certifie all the Queenes Majesties officers and lovinge subjects, to whom theise presents shall come, that the bearer, Alice Stynton, the wief of John Stynton, of the towne of Leycester, pettye chapman, dothe dwell and inhabyte in the parish of St. Nicholas, in the said town, in a streete called the Sore Laine, neyre unto the West Brigge.

The which John Stynton hathe not bene in Leycester sythence one fortnytt after St. James Daye last; but travelinge abrode in Northamptonshier about his lawfull affaires in gaytheringe under the Greate Seale of England, by lycence, for a poore house at Waltam Crosse.

And this bearer, his wief, with hym all the said tyme, untill her nowe comyng hom to Leycester, which was aboute a weeke past. The which bearer her dwellyng ys not neyre unto places suspected of the plage, but ys cleyre and sound from the same, God be thancked, neyther ys there any att this present sicke thereof in the said streete or parish, God be praised. Do therefore request you to permytt and suffer her quietlye to travell to her husband, and also to permytt and suffer her said husband and her quietlye, upon ther honest behavire, to travell aboute ther lawfull busynes withoute any your hyndrance, and you the constables to helpe them to lodginges in ther said travell yf such nede shall require. In witnes whereof, we the mayor and alderman of the saide towne of Leycester have hereunto subscribed our names, and sette the seale of office of the said mayor, this vj[th] daye of October 1593, A° 35° Eliz."

The records of Beverley supply some important notes respecting persons leaving the place. We gather from George Oliver's history of Beverley, that the plague raged with great violence in the year 1610, death and desertion were greatly thinning the town; the corporation made an order, directing that a fine of ten shillings be imposed on every individual leaving the town, even to go to fairs and markets, without the mayor's special permission. If the preceding measure was insufficient to detain persons in Beverley, it was resolved to imprison or otherwise punish, at the discretion of the justices, those offending.

The head of every family had to report periodically, during the time of the plague, to the constable in his ward, the state of the health of his household. If the disease attacked any member of his family, or those under his charge, and he neglected, within a specified number of hours, to report the matter, he was liable to a fine of forty shillings, to be placed in the town's chest.

The town of Derby suffered greatly from a plague in 1592-3. It appears to have been imported in some bales of cloth from the Levant to London, and quickly spread into the provinces. In the parish register of St. Alkmund's, Derby, under October, 1592, is this statement, " Hic

M

incipit pestis prestifera." It took twelve months
to run its destructive course.

The register of All Saints', Derby, under
October, 1593, says: "About this time, the
plague of pestilence, by the great mercy and
goodness of Almighty God, stay'd, past all
expectac'on of man, for it rested upon assondaye,
at what tyme it was dispersed in every corner of
this whole p'she: ther was not two houses
together free from ytt, and yet the Lord bade his
angell staye, as in Davide's tyme: His name be
blessed for ytt."

The inhabitants of Derby suffered greatly from
a plague in 1665. In the Arboretum of the town
is a memorial of the visitation, in the form of a
stone, bearing the following inscription :

### "Ibeadless Cross, or
### *MARKET STONE.*

Ubis Stone FORMED PART OF AN ANCIENT CROSS AT THE
UPPER END OF FRIAR GATE, AND WAS USED BY THE
INHABITANTS OF DERBY AS A MARKET STONE DURING
THE VISITATION OF THE PLAGUE, 1665. IT IS THUS DESCRIBED
BY HUTTON IN HIS HISTORY OF DERBY.

---

'1665. Derby was again visited by the plague at the same
time in which London fell under that severe calamity. The
town was forsaken; the farmers declined the Market-place;
and grass grew upon that spot which had furnished the
supports of life. To prevent a famine, the inhabitants

erected at the top of Nuns-green, one or two hundred yards from the buildings, now Friar-gate, what bore the name of *Headless-cross*, consisting of about four quadrangular steps, covered in the centre with one large stone; the whole near five feet high; I knew it in perfection. Hither the market-people, having their mouths primed with tobacco as a preservative, brought their provisions, stood at a distance from their property, and at a greater from the townspeople, with whom they were to traffic. 'The buyer was not suffered to touch any of the articles before purchase; but when the agreement was finished, he took the goods, and deposited the money in a vessel filled with vinegar, set for that purpose.'"

Tobacco has long been regarded as an efficacious preservative against disease. There is a curious entry in Thomas Hearne's Diary, 1720-21, bearing on this matter. He thus writes, under date of January 21st: "I have been told that in the last great plague in London none that kept tobacconists' shops had the plague. It is certain that smoking was looked upon as a most excellent preservative. In so much, that even children were obliged to smoak. And I remember that I heard formerly Tom Rogers, who was yeoman beadle, say that, when he was that year, when the plague raged, a school-boy at Eaton, all the boys of that school were obliged to smoak in the school every morning, and that he was never whipped so much in his life as he was one morning for not smoaking."

Charles Knight, in his "Old England," gives
an original drawing of the Broad Stone, East
Retford, Nottinghamshire.   He says, on this
stone, money, previously immersed in vinegar,

THE BROAD STONE, EAST RETFORD.

was placed in exchange for goods, during the
Great Plague.

In front of Tothby House, near Alford,
Lincolnshire, under a spreading tree, is a large
stone, which formerly stood on Miles Cross Hill,
and, when the town was plague-stricken, in the

year 1630, on this stone, money immersed in vinegar was deposited, in exchange for food brought from Spilsby and other places. From July 22nd, 1630, to the end of February, 1631, 132 burials are recorded in the parish register, and this out of a population of under 1000 persons, a proportion equal to that of London during the Great Plague. In one homestead, within twelve days, were six deaths. The Rev. Geo. S. Tyack, B.A., who has contributed a carefully-prepared chapter to " Bygone Lincolnshire " on this theme, does not state how the scourge was brought to Alford.

The dead were, as a rule, buried at night, without coffin and ceremony, and frequently in a common grave outside the usual graveyards, like, for example, those in the pest pit of London. " Bring out your dead! Bring out your dead!" was the dismal cry which was heard in London during the Great Plague. The people were dead and buried in a few hours, and it is believed that many were interred alive. A well-known instance occurred at Stratford-on-Avon. The plague raged at the town in 1564, and swept away one-seventh of the inhabitants. The council chamber was closed, but the councillors did not neglect

their duties ; they met in a garden to discuss the
best means of helping the sufferers.   The visitation was not confined only to the homes of the
poor.   The Manor House of Clopton was attacked,
and one of its fair inmates, a beautiful girl named
Charlotte Clopton, was sick, and to all appearance
died.   She was buried without delay in the family
vault, underneath Stratford Church.   A week
passed, and another was borne to the same resting
place.   When the vault was opened, a terrible
sight was presented.   Charlotte Clopton was seen
leaning against the wall in her grave clothes.
She had been buried alive, and, on recovering
from the plague, had attempted to get out of the
vault, when death had ended her sufferings.

At Bradley, in the parish of Malpas, Cheshire,
an entire family, named Dawson, consisting of
seven members and two servants, died of the
plague, in the year 1625.   One of Dawson's sons
had been in London, and returned home sick,
died, and infected the whole household.   The
deaths commenced towards the end of July and
ended September 15th.   Respecting Richard
Dawson, the following particulars are given in the
parish register, after stating that he was the brother
of the head of the house : " being sicke of the

plague, and perceyving he must die at yt time, arose
out of his bed and made his grave, and caused his
nefew, John Dawson, to cast strawe into the grave,
w'ch was not farre from the house, and went and
lay'd him down in the say'd grave, and caused
clothes to be layd uppon, and so dep'ted out of
this world; this he did, because he was a strong
man, and heavier than his said nefew and another
wench were able to bury.    He died about xxivth
of August.   Thus much I was credibly tould he
did."   The next entry in this distressing record
bears date of August 29th, and is that of the
nephew just named, and, on September 15th, Rose
Smyth, the servant, doubtless the wench referred
to, was buried, "and the last of yt household."

At Braintree, in Essex, in 1665, the plague
made great ravages.   In that year, 665 persons
died of it, being fully one-third of the inhabitants
of the place.   Business was at a standstill, the
town was shunned, and the inhabitants had to
depend on charity.   Long grass grew in the
streets, and the whole place was one of desolation.
At this time, Dr. Kidder, afterwards Bishop of
Bath and Wells, was looking after the spiritual
welfare of the place.   His life contains a painful
picture of the sufferings of the inhabitants.   In

his own house, a young gentleman was attacked and died. "My neighbours," he writes, "durst not come near, and the provisions which were procured for us were laid at a distance, upon a green before my house. No tongue can express the dismal calamity which that part of Essex lay under at that time. As for myself, I was in perpetual danger. I conversed daily with those who came from the infected houses, and it was unavoidable. The provisions sent into the neighbouring infected town were left at the village where I was, and near my house. Thither the Earl of Warwick sent his fat bullocks, which he did every week give to the poor of Braintree. The servants were not willing to carry them further. This occasioned frequent coming from that infected place to my village, and, indeed, to my very door. My parish clerk had it when he put on my surplice, and went from me to his house, and died. Another neighbour had three children, and they all died in three nights immediately succeeding each other, and I was forced to carry them to the churchyard and bury them. We were alarmed perpetually with the news of the death of our neighbours and acquaintances, and awakened to expect our turns.

This continued a great part of the summer. It pleased God to preserve me and mine from this noisome pestilence. Praised be his name." The plague at Colchester, in the same county, in 1665-6, made the death rate higher than that of the neighbouring town or even of London. Its deadly operations opened in August, 1665, and closed in December, 1666, and, in that period, passed away 4,731 persons. Poverty prevailed, but help poured in from many places. Weekly collections were made in the churches of London, and by this means the sum of £1,311 10s. was obtained. The oath book of the Corporation contains the form of oath administered to men known as "Searchers of the Plague." It was the duty of the men to search out and view the corpses of all who died, and, in cases of death from the plague, to make known the fact to the constables of the parish, and the bearers appointed to bury them. The searchers had to live together, and apart from their families, and not go abroad, except in execution of their duty. They were careful not to go near any one, and they carried in their hands white wands, so that people might know them and so avoid them.

Collections in churches were very general for

those suffering from the plague. The following
entry, reproduced from the parish register of the
small town of Cheadle, Staffordshire, may be
quoted as a specimen of similar records :

> " 1666. Collected on the first
> monthly fast, being second day
> of August, towards the relief of
> the persons and places visited
> by the plague ..................... 14s. 7d."

The plague penetrated into most unexpected
places. Far away from London, in the Peak of
Derbyshire, is the delightfully-situated mountain
village of Eyam, a place swept over by health-
giving breezes. It is a locality of apparent
security against infection. In September, 1665,
a parcel of tailor's patterns was sent from London
to Eyam, and with it came the disease. At that
time the village had a population of 350 persons,
and when the plague "was exhausted with
excessive slaughter," only seventy-three were
alive. From September 6th, 1665, to October
11th, 1666, 277 died, the death rate being much
higher than that of London. The history of this
visitation is heart-rending, and has been told by
several writers, but by none more carefully than
by William Wood, in his "History of Eyam,"

published by Richard Keene, of Derby. Two names in this dark story stand out in bright relief, one was the Rev. Thomas Stanley, the ejected rector of the parish, in 1662, and the Rev. William Mompesson, a successor, who was appointed in 1664. With their lives in their hands, these two brave men remained at the post of duty, visited, advised, and aided the sufferers unto death. Mrs. Mompesson administered daily to her husband's suffering parishioners until death closed her useful life, on the 24th August, 1666. This was a terrible blow to her devoted husband, and a heavy loss to the villagers. "At one time," we are told, " Mrs. Mompesson's heart failed her, when she thought of her two children in the midst of the plague. She cast herself and her two children at the feet of her husband, and begged that they might all depart from the death-stricken place. In the most loving manner, however, he raised her from his feet, and pointed out the awful responsibility which would attach to his deserting his post. He then besought his wife to flee to some distant spot, where she and her babes might be safe. She refused, however, to leave him, but they mutually agreed to send the children to a relative in Yorkshire."

About the middle of June, the more wealthy
people fled to distant places from the plague-
stricken village, and others built huts on the
neighbouring hills, and in them took shelter.
The entire population appeared determined to
flee.    Mr. Mompesson pointed out the folly of
such a proceeding, observing that they would
carry the disease to other places.    His earnest
entreaties prevailed.

He wrote to the Earl of Devonshire for
assistance, to enable the inhabitants to remain in
their own village.    The Earl realised the
importance of confining the disease within a
certain limit.    He readily made arrangements for
a constant supply of food and clothing for the
sufferers.    A boundary was fixed round the
village, marked by stones, and the residents
solemnly agreed that not one should go beyond
the radius indicated.    The provisions, etc., were
left early in the morning at an appointed place,
and were fetched away by men selected for the
work.    If money was paid, it was placed in water.
The men of Eyam faithfully kept their promise,
so that the plague was not carried by them to any
other places.

The churchyard was closed and funeral rites

were not read ; graves were made in fields and gardens near the cottages of the departed.

During the time the disease was at its height, the church was closed but the faithful rector did not neglect to assemble his flock each succeeding Sabbath in a quiet spot on the south side of the village, and to proclaim to them words of comfort.

Shortly after the disease had stopped at Eyam, the rectory of Eaking was presented to Mr. Mompesson. The inhabitants of his new parish had such a terror of the plague that they dreaded his coming amongst them, and a hut was built for him in Rufford Park, where he remained until their fears had subsided.

This short study of a serious subject enables us to fully realise the force of the supplication in the Litany : " From Plague and Pestilence, Good Lord deliver us."

## A King Curing an Abbot of Indigestion.

MANY of the English monarchs have
delighted in the pleasures of the
chase. Their hunting expeditions
have often led them into out-of-the-way places
where they were unknown, and their adventures
gave rise to good stories, which have done much
to enliven the dry pages of national history.
Bluff King Hal was a jovial huntsman, and was
one day enjoying the pastime in the glades of
Windsor Forest, when he missed his way, and, to
his surprise, found himself near the Abbey at
Reading. He keenly felt the pangs of hunger,
and resolved to try and get a meal at the table of
the Abbey hard by.

After disguising himself, he made his way to
the house, under the pretence of being one of the
king's guards. He was invited to partake of a
sirloin of beef, and he did such justice to it as to

surprise not a little the worthy abbot. The latter pledged his guest's royal master, adding that if his weak stomach could digest such a meal as his visitor had just eaten he would gladly give a hundred pounds. He lamented that he could only take for his dinner the wing of a chicken, or other equally small dainty. The burly stranger pledged him in return, and, after expressing his gratitude, departed without his identity being discovered.

After a few short weeks had passed, another stranger wended his way to the Abbey of Reading, armed with a warrant from King Henry VIII. to take the abbot a prisoner, and lodge him in the Tower. It was with a heavy heart that the abbot journeyed to London. His prison fare was very plain, and consisted of bread and water, and provided in small quantities, so that he not only suffered in mind, but also from the want of food. He often wondered what he had done to displease the king, but could not obtain any information on the subject. A change at last came over the scene. A fine sirloin of beef was placed on his table, and he was bidden to feast to his heart's content. He did not need any pressing to do justice to the joint, for he was almost famished, and dined more like a glutton than a man with a weak stomach. The king watched with amusement, from a secret place, the abbot enjoying his dinner, and, when he had nearly completed it, stepped forth from his hiding place, and demanded one hundred pounds for curing the poor abbot of his indigestion, and reminded him of their former meeting at the Abbey of Reading. The patient gladly paid his physician the stipulated fee, and, with a light purse and a merry heart, bent his steps homeward.

## The Services and Customs of Royal Oak Day.

RITING in his diary, on May 29th, 1665, John Evelyn says: "This was the first anniversary appointed by Act of Parliament to be observed as a day of General Thanksgiving for the miraculous restoration of his Majesty: our vicar preaching on Psalm cxviii. 24, requiring us to be thankful and rejoice, as indeed we had cause." A special form of prayer in commemoration of the Restoration of Charles II. was included in the Book of Common Prayer until 1859, when it was removed by Act of Parliament.

On this day, the Chaplain of the House of Commons used to preach before the House, in St. Margaret's Church, Westminster. The service has been discontinued since 1858. It attracted little attention, and the congregation usually consisted of the Speaker, the Sergeant-at-arms, the clerks and other officers, and about half a dozen members.

It was, in bygone times, in many parts of England, the practice, on this day, to fasten boughs of oak to the pinnacles of church steeples.

The display of oak is in memory of the king's escape after the Battle of Worcester, in 1651, and of his successfully hiding himself in an oak tree at Boscobel. Tennyson, in his "Talking Oak," refers to the subject :

> " Thy famous brother oak,
> Wherein the younger Charles abode,
>     Till all the paths grew dim,
> While far below the Roundheads rode,
>     And humm'd a surly hymn."

Richard Penderel greatly assisted Charles in his time of trouble, and he selected the oak in which safety was found. When Charles "came to his own," the claims of Penderel were not overlooked. He was attached to the Court. When he died, he was buried with honours at St. Giles-in-the-Fields. It was customary, for a long period, to decorate his grave in the churchyard with oak branches.

Formerly, in Derbyshire, it was the practice to

place over the doors of houses, branches of young oak, and it is still the custom for boys to wear sprigs of the same tree in their hats and button-holes. If the lads neglect to wear the oak-leaf they are stung with nettles by their more loyal companions. At Looe, and other districts of East Cornwall, it was enforced by spitting at or "cobbing" the offender. In bygone times, the boys of Newcastle-on-Tyne had an insulting rhyme, which they used to repeat to such folk as they met who did not wear oak-leaves :

> " Royal oak
> The Whigs to provoke."

On this day, many wore plane tree leaves, and would make a retort to the foregoing rhyme :

> " Plane tree leaves ;
> The Church folk are thieves."

Mr. John Nicholson, in his " Folk Lore of East Yorkshire " (Hull, 1890), has an interesting note on this subject. " During the days of spring," says Mr. Nicholson, " boys busily ' bird-nest ' (seek nests), and lay up a store of eggs for the 29th of May, Royal Oak Day, or Mobbing Day. These eggs are expended by being thrown at other boys, but all boys who carry a sprig of Royal Oak, not dog oak, either in their cap or

coat, are free from molestation. Not only wild
birds' eggs, but the eggs of hens and ducks are
used to 'mob' (pelt) with, and the older and more
unsavoury the eggs are, the better are they liked
—by the thrower. The children sing :

> ' The twenty-ninth of May,
> Royal Oak Day,
> If you don't give us a holiday
> We'll all run away.' "

At Castleton, Derbyshire, an old custom still
lingers of making a huge garland of flowers on
this day, and afterwards suspending it on the
top of the principal pinnacle of the church. The
late Mr. Alfred Burton saw this garland constructed
in 1885, and had a drawing made of it for his
volume entitled " Rush-bearing." " The framework," says Mr. Burton, "is of wood, thatched
with straw. Interior diameter, a little over two
feet, outside (when covered with flowers), over
three feet six inches. In shape it somewhat
resembles a bell, completely covered over with
wild flowers—hyacinths, water-buttercups, butter-
cups, daisies, forget-me-nots, wallflowers,
rhododendrons, tulips, and ornamental grasses,
in rows, each composed of the same flower, which
have been gathered in the neighbourhood the

evening before. The top, called the 'queen,'
is formed of garden flowers, and fits into a
socket at the top of the garland. It weighs
over a hundredweight, requires two men to lift it,
and has occupied four men from noon till five
o'clock in the afternoon to make it."

CASTLETON GARLAND.

At six in the evening, a procession is formed
from a village inn, whose turn it is to take the
lead in the festivities. A band of music heads
the processionists, next comes the garland, which,
we are told by Mr. Burton, is "borne on the head

and shoulders of a man riding a horse, and wearing a red jacket.  A stout handle inside, which rests on the saddle in front of him, enables him to hold it upright.  It completely envelopes him to the waist, and is roomy enough to enable ale to be passed up to his mouth, of which he takes good care to have a share.  His horse is led for him, and he is followed by another man on horseback, dressed as a woman, who acts the fool. These are followed by the villagers, dancing, even old people who can scarcely walk making a point of attempting to dance on this, the greatest day in the year at Castleton.  After parading the village, the 'queen' is taken off the garland and placed in the church, the garland being hoisted with ropes to the top of the church tower, where it is placed on one of the pinnacles, and left till it has withered away, when the framework is taken down and kept for another year. The other pinnacles have branches of oak."

In the churchwardens' accounts of Castleton, are entries as follows :

"1749.   Pd. for an iron rod to hang
singers' garland on .............. 0 0 8.
1750.   Pd. ringers on 29th May... 0 3 0."
Payments for ringing bells on the 29th May

occur frequently in churchwardens' accounts, and a few examples may be quoted. The first is from Wellington, Somerset:

" 1688.   Pd. for ringing, the 29th
       May ............................. o 5 o."

The accounts of St. Michael's, Bishop Stortford, state:

" 1703.   Pd. ringers 29th May ...... o 6 8."

St. Mary's, Stamford, contain an item as follows:

" 1709.   Pd. Richard Hambleton
       for ale for the ringers on ye
       29th May ................... oo o6 o8."

Northampton is loyal to the memory of Charles II. He was a benefactor to the borough, and helped the inhabitants after the great fire of 1675. In the Baptismal Register of All Saints', Northampton, it is recorded, under September 1675, as follows: "In this month, a very lamentable fire destroyed 3 parts of our Towne and Church." The Marriage Register says: "While the world lasts, remember September the 20th, a dreadfull fire, it consumed to ashes in a few houres, 3 parts of our Towne and Cheef Church." The sum of £25,000 was collected by briefs and private charities towards the heavy loss sustained by the inhabitants. Charles II. gave 1000 tons of timber out of Whittlewood forest, and remitted the duty of chimney-money in the town for seven years.   We gather from Hume, that "the king's debts had become so intolerable, that the commons were constrained to vote him an extraordinary supply of £1,200,000, to be levied by eighteen months' assessment, and, finding upon inquiry that the several branches of the revenue fell much short of the sums they expected, they at last, after much delay, voted a new imposition of 2s. on each hearth, and this tax they settled on the king during his life."

Macaulay speaks of this tax as being "peculiarly odious, for it could only be levied by means of domiciliary visits. . . . The poorer householders were frequently unable to pay their hearth-money to the day.   When this happened, their furniture was distrained without mercy, for the tax was farmed, and a farmer of taxes, is, of all creditors, proverbially, the most rapacious."   He quotes from some doggerel ballads of the period, and the following is one of the verses reproduced :

> "The good old dames, whenever they the chimney-man
>    espied,
>   Unto their nooks they haste away, their pots and pipkins
>    hide ;

" There is not one old dame in ten, and search the nation
  through,
  But, if you talk of chimney-men, will spare a curse or
  two."

A reference to chimney-money occurs in an
epitaph in Folkestone churchyard. Here is a
copy :

" In Memory of

R EBECCA   R OGERS,

who died August 22nd, 1688.

Aged 44 years.

A house she hath ; it's made of such good fashion,
The tenant ne'er shall pay for reparation,
Nor will her landlord ever raise her rent,
Or turn her out of doors for non-payment.
From chimney-money too this cell is free—
To such a house, who would not tenant be ?"

The inhabitants of Northampton, to show
their gratitude to the king for his consideration,
displayed oak branches over their house doors.
The members of the corporation, accompanied by
the children of the charity schools, attend service
at All Saints' Church. A statue of the king, in
front of the church, is usually enveloped in
oak boughs on May 29th.

## Marrying in a White Sheet.

IT was not an uncommon circumstance in the last, and even in the early years of the present century, for marriages to be performed *en chemise*, or in a white sheet. It was an old belief, that a man marrying a woman in debt, if he received her at the hands of the minister clothed only in her shift, was not liable to pay the accounts she had contracted before their union. We think it will not be without interest to give a few authenticated instances of this class of marriages.

The earliest example we have found, is recorded in the parish register of Chiltern, All Saints', Wilts. It is stated: "John Bridmore and Anne Selwood were married October 17th, 1714. The aforesaid Anne Selwood was married in her smock, without any clothes or headgier on."

On June 25th, 1738, George Walker, a linen weaver, and Mary Gee, of the "George and Dragon," Gorton Green, were made man and wife, at the ancient chapel close by. The bride was only attired in her shift.

Particulars of another local case are given in the columns of *Harrop's Manchester Mercury*, for March 12th, 1771, as follows : "On Thursday last, was married, at Ashton-under-Lyne, Nathaniel Eller to the widow Hibbert, both upwards of fifty years of age ; the widow had only her shift on, with her hair tied behind with horse hair, as a means to free them both from any obligation of paying her former husband's debts."

We have heard of a case where the vicar declined to marry a couple on account of the woman presenting herself in her under garment. Another clergyman, after carefully reading the rubric, and not finding anything about the bride's dress, married a pair, although the woman wore only her chemise.

The following is taken from *Aris's Birmingham Gazette* for 1797 :

"There is an opinion generally prevalent in Staffordshire that if a woman should marry a man in distressed circumstances, none of his creditors can touch her property if she should be in *puris naturalibus* while the ceremony is performed. In consequence of this prejudice, a woman of some property lately came with her intended husband into the vestry of the great church of Birmingham, and the moment she understood the priest was ready at the altar, she threw off a large cloak, and in the exact state of Eve in Paradise, walked deliberately to the spot, and remained in that state till the ceremony was ended. This circumstance has naturally excited much noise in the neighbourhood, and various opinions prevail respecting the conduct of the clergyman. Some vehemently condemn him as having given sanction to an act of indecency; and others think, as nothing is said relative to dress in the nuptial ceremony, that he had no power to refuse the rite. Our readers may be assured of this extraordinary event, however improbable it may appear in these times of virtue and decorum."

We gather from a periodical called *The Athenian*, that this custom was practised in Yorkshire at the beginning of this century: "May, 1808. At Otley, in Yorkshire, Mr. George Rastrick, of Hawkesworth, aged 73, to

Mrs. Nulton, of Burley Woodhead, aged 60. In compliance with the vulgar notion that a wife being married in a state of nudity exonerated her husband from legal obligations to discharge any demands on her purse, the bride disrobed herself at the altar, and stood shivering in her chemise while the marriage ceremony was performed."

In Lincolnshire, at so late a period as between 1838 and 1844, a woman was wed enveloped in a sheet.

A slightly different method of marriage is mentioned in Malcolm's "Anecdotes of London." It is stated that "a brewer's servant, in February, 1723, to prevent his liability to the payment of the debts of a Mrs. Brittain, whom he intended to marry, the lady made her appearance at the door of St. Clement Danes habited in her shift; hence her inamorato conveyed the modest fair to a neighbouring apothecary's, where she was completely equipped with clothing purchased by him; and in these, Mrs. Brittain changed her name in church."

In the foregoing, it will have been observed that the marriages have been conducted *en chemise* for the protection of the pocket of the bridegroom. "The Annual Register," of 1766,

contains an account of a wedding of this
class, for the protection of the woman. We
read : " A few days ago, a handsome, well-dressed
young woman came to a church in Whitehaven,
to be married to a man, who was attending there
with the clergyman. When she had advanced a
little into the church, a nymph, her bridesmaid,
began to undress her, and, by degrees, stript her
to her shift ; thus she was led, blooming and
unadorned, to the altar, where the marriage
ceremony was performed. It seems this droll
wedding was occasioned by an embarrassment in
the affairs of the intended husband, upon which
account the girl was advised to do this, that he
might be entitled to no other marriage portion
than her smock."

## Marrying under the Gallows.

SOME of the old ballads of merry England contain allusions to a law or usage of primitive times, to the effect that if a man or woman would consent to marry, under the gallows, a person condemned to death, the criminal would escape hanging. A few criminals, however, preferred the hangman's knot to the marriage tie, if we may believe the rude rhymes of our ancestors. In one of Pinkerton's works may be read an old poem in which we are told of a criminal refusing marriage at the foot of the gallows. Here are a few lines from the ballad :

> " There was a victim in a cart,
> One day for to be hanged,
> And his reprieve was granted,
> And the cart made a stand.

> " ' Come, marry a wife and save your life,'
>     The judge aloud did cry ;
> ' Oh, why should I corrupt my life '
>     The victim did reply.

> ' For here's a crowd of every sort,
>     And why should I prevent their sport !
> The bargain's bad in every part,
>     The wife's the worst—drive on the cart ?' "

A poem, published in 1542, entitled the " Schole House," contains an allusion :

> " To hang or wed, both hath one home,
>     And whether it be, I am well sure
> Hangynge is better of the twayne—
>     Sooner done, and shorter payne."

We read in an old ballad the story of a merchant of Chichester, who was saved execution by a loving maiden.

In the old Manx " Temporal Customary Laws," A.D. 1577, occurs the following : " If any man take a woman by constraint, or force her against her will, if she be a wife he must suffer the law of her. If she be a maid or single woman, the deemster shall give her a rope, sword, and a ring, and she shall have her choice to hang him with the rope, cut off his head with the sword, or marry him with the ring !"

It is stated in a work published in 1680, entitled

"Warning to Servants, or, the case of Margaret Clark, lately executed for firing her master's house in Southwark." "Since the poor maid was executed, there has been a false and malicious story published concerning her in the *True Domestick Intelligence* of Tuesday, March 30th. There was omitted in the confession of Mary Clark (so he falsely calls her), who was executed for firing the house of M. de la Noy, dyer in Southwark, viz., that, at her execution, there was a fellow who designed to marry her under the gallows (according to the antient laudable custome), but she, being in hopes of a reprieve, seemed unwilling; but, when the rope was about her neck, she cryed she was willing, and then the fellow's friends dissuaded him from marrying her; so she lost her husband and life together." To the foregoing is added, "We know of no such custome allowed by law, that any man's offering, at a place of execution, to marry a woman condemned shall save her."

Here is a curious paragraph bearing on this theme, drawn from *Parker's London News*, for April 7th, 1725: "Nine young women dressed in white, each with a white wand in her hand, presented a petition to his Majesty (George I.) on behalf of a young man condemned at Kingston

Assizes of burglary, one of them offered to marry him under the gallows in case of a reprieve."

In a work entitled " The interesting narrative of the life of Oulandah Equians, or Gustavus Vassa, written by himself," and published in 1789, is the following passage : " While we lay here (New York, 1784) a circumstance happened which I thought extremely singular. One day, a malefactor was to be executed on the gallows, but with the condition that if any woman, having nothing on but her shift, married a man under the gallows, his life would be saved. This extraordinary privilege was claimed ; and a woman presented herself, and the marriage ceremony was performed."

## Kissing the Bride.

THE parents of a bride in humble circumstances rarely attend the marriage ceremony at the church. The father's place is usually filled by one of the bridegroom's friends. He, in some parts of the North of England, claims the privilege of first kissing the newly-made wife, in right of his temporary paternity. Some of the old-fashioned clergy regarded the prerogative as theirs, and were by no means slow in exercising it. As soon as the ceremony was completed they never failed to quickly kiss the bride. Even a shy and retiring vicar would not neglect the pleasant duty. The Rev. Thomas Ebdon, vicar of Merrington, who was deemed the most bashful of men, always kissed the women he married.

It is related of a priest, who was a stranger to the manners and customs of the Yorkshire folk,

that, after marrying a couple, he was surprised to
see the party still standing as if something more
was expected.    He at last asked why they were
waiting.    " Please, sir," said the bridegroom,
"ye've no kissed Molly."

Mr. William Henderson, in his ." Folk-Lore of
the Northern Counties," a work drawn upon for
these statements, says that he can " testify that,
within the last ten years, a fair lady, from the
county of Durham, who was married in the south
of England, so undoubtedly reckoned upon the
clerical salute that, after waiting in vain, she
boldly took the initiative, and bestowed a kiss on
the   much-amazed   south-country   vicar."    Mr.
Henderson's work was published in 1879.

According to the " Folk-Lore of the West of
Scotland," by James Napier, published in 1879,
the   kissing   custom   was   practised   in   that
country.    "As soon as the ceremony was concluded," says Mr. Napier, "there was a rush on
the part of young men to get the first kiss of the
newly-made wife.    This was frequently taken by
the clergyman himself, a survival of an old custom
said to have been practised in the middle ages."
In an old song, the bridegroom thus addresses
the minister :

" It's no very decent for you to be kissing,
  It does not look well wi' the black coat ava',
'Twould hae set you far better tae gi'en us your blessing,
  Than thus by such tricks to be breaking the law.
Dear Watty, quo' Robin, it's just an auld custom,
  And the thing that is common should ne'er be ill taen,
For where ye are wrong, if ye hadna a wished him,
  You should have been first.   It's yoursel it's to blame."

This custom appears to have been very general
in past times, and Mr. Henderson suggests that
"it may possibly be a dim memorial of the
*osculum pacis*, or the presentation of the Pax to
the newly-married pair."

It was formerly customary in Ireland for the
priest to conclude the marriage ceremony by
saying, "kiss your wife." Instructions more
easily given than performed, for other members
of the party did their utmost to give the first
salute.

In England, a kiss was the established
fee for a lady's partner after the dance was
finished. In a " Dialouge between Custom and
Veirtie concerning the Use and Abuse of Dancing
and Minstrelsie," the following appears :

" But some reply, what foole would daunce,
    If that when daunce is doone
  He may not have at ladye's lips
    That which in daunce he woon ? "

The following line occurs in the *Tempest* :

"Curtsied when you have and kissed."

In *Henry VIII.*, says the prince :

"I were unmannerly to take you out,
And not to kiss you."

Numerous other references to kissing are contained in the plays of Shakespeare. From his works and other sources we find that kissing was general in the country in the olden time. It is related of Sir William Cavendish, the biographer of Cardinal Wolsey, that, when he visited a French nobleman at his chateau, his hostess, on entering the room with her train of attendant maidens, for the purpose of welcoming the visitor, thus accosted him :

"Forasmuch as ye be an Englishman, whose custom it is in your country to kiss all ladies and gentlemen without offence, it is not so in this realm, yet will I be so bold as to kiss you, and so shall all my maidens."

It is further stated how Cavendish was delighted to salute the fair hostess and her many merry maidens.

## Hot Ale at Weddings.

IN the year 1891, a paragraph went the rounds of the north-country newspapers respecting the maintaining of an old wedding custom at Whitburn parish church, near Sunderland. From the days of old to the present time, it has been the practice of sending to the church porch, when a marriage is being solemnised, jugs of spiced ale, locally known as "hot pots."

A Whitburn gentleman supplied Mr. Henderson with particulars of his wedding, for insertion in "Folk-Lore of the Northern Counties" (London, 1879). "After the vestry scene," says the correspondent, "the bridal party having formed a procession for leaving the church, we were stopped at the porch by a row of five or six women, ranged to our left hand, each holding a large mug with a cloth over it. These were in turn presented to me, and handed by me to my wife, who, after taking a sip, returned it to me. It was then passed to the next couple, and so on in the same form to all the party. The composition in these mugs was mostly, I am sorry to say, simply horrible; one or two were very fair, one very good. They are sent to the church by all classes, and are considered a great compliment. I have never heard of this custom elsewhere. Here, it has existed beyond the memory of the oldest inhabitant, and an aged fisherwoman, who has been married some sixty-five years, tells me at her wedding there were seventy hot pots."

Drinking wine and ale at church weddings is by no means a local custom, as suggested by Mr. Henderson's correspondent. Brand, in his " Popular Antiquities," and other writers, refer to the subject. On drinking wine in church at marriages, says Brand, "the custom is enjoined in the Hereford Missal. By the Sarum Missal it is directed that the sops immersed in this wine, as well as the liquor itself, and the cup that contained it, should be blessed by the priest. The beverage used on this occasion was to be drunk by the bride and bridegroom and the rest of the company." It appears that pieces of cake or wafers were immersed in the wine, hence the allusions to sops.

Many of the older poets refer to the practice. In the works of John Heywood, "newlie imprinted 1576," is a passage as follows :

"The drinke of my brydecup I should have forborne,
Till temperaunce had tempred the taste beforne.
I see now, and shall see, while I am alive,
Who wedth or he be wise shall die or he thrive."

In the "Compleat Vintner," 1720, it is asked :

"What priest can join two lovers' hands,
But wine must seal the marriage bands?
As if celestial wine was thought
Essential to the sacred knot,
And that each bridegroom and his bride
Believ'd they were not firmly ty'd
Till Bacchus, with his bleeding tun,
Had finished what the priest begun."

Old plays contain allusions to this custom. We read in Dekker's "Satiro-Mastix": "And, when we are at church, bring the wine and cakes." Beaumont and Fletcher, in the "Scornful Lady," say :

"If my wedding-smock were on,
Were the gloves bought and given, the licence come,
Were the rosemary branches dipt, and all
The hippocras and cakes eat and drunk off."

At the magnificent marriage of Queen Mary

and Philip, in Winchester Cathedral, in 1554, we are told that, "The trumpets sounded, and they both returned, hand in hand, to their traverses in the quire, and there remained until mass was done, at which time wyne and sopes were hallowed, and delivered to them both."

Numerous other notes similar to the foregoing might be reproduced from old writers, but sufficient have been cited to show how general was the custom in bygone times. The Rev. W. Carr, in his "Glossary of the Craven Dialect," gives us an illustration of it lingering in another form in the present century. In his definition of Bride-ale, he observes that after the ceremony was concluded at the church, there took place either a foot or horse race, the first to arrive at the dwelling of the bride, "requested to be shown to the chamber of the newly-married pair, then, after he had turned down the bed-clothes, he returns, carrying in his hand a tankard of warm ale, previously prepared, to meet the bride, to whom he triumphantly offers the humble beverage." The bride, in return for this, presents to him a ribbon as his reward.

## Marrying Children.

THE marriage of children forms a curious feature in old English life. In the days of yore, to use the words of a well-informed writer on this theme, " babes were often mated in the cradle, ringed in the nursery, and brought to the church porch with lollipops in their mouths." Parents and guardians frequently had joined together in matrimony young couples, without any regard for their feelings. Down to the days of James I., the disposal in marriage of young orphan heiresses was in the hands of the reigning monarchs, and they usually arranged to wed them to the sons of their favourites, by whom unions with wealthy girls were welcomed.

Edward I. favoured early marriages, and his ninth daughter, Eleanor, was only four days old, it is stated on good authority, "when her father

arranged to espouse her to the son and heir of
Otho, late Earl of Burgundy and Artois, a
child in custody of his mother, the Duchess of
Burgundy." Before she had reached the age of
a year, the little princess was a spouse, but, dying
in her sixth year, she did not attain the position
of wife planned for her.

Careful consideration is paid to early marriages
in an able work by the late Rev. W. Denton, M.A.,
entitled "England in the Fifteenth Century"
(London, 1888.) Mr. Denton says that the
youthful marriages "probably originated in the
desire of anticipating the Crown in its claim to
the wardship of minors, and the disposal of them
in marriage. As deaths were early in those days,
and wardship frequent, a father sought by the
early marriage of his son or daughter to dispose
of their hands in his lifetime, instead of leaving
them to be dealt out to hungry courtiers, who
only sought to make a large profit, as they could,
from the marriage of wards they had bought for
the purpose. Fourteen was a usual period for
the marriage of the children of those who would
save their lands from the exactions of the Crown."
He adverts to marriages at an earlier age, and
even paternity at fourteen.

In 1583 was published a work entitled "The Anatomie of Abuses," by Philip Stubbes, and it supplies a curious account of the amusements and other social customs of the day. Marriage comes in for attention, and, after referring to it with words of commendation, he adds: "There is permitted one great liberty therein—for little maids in swaddling clothes are often married by their ambitious parents and friends, when they know neither good nor evil, and this is the origin of much wickedness. And, besides this, you shall have a saucy boy often, fourteen, sixteen, or twenty years of age, catch up a woman without any fear of God at all." The protests of Stubbes and others had little effect, for children continued to be married, if not mated.

The marriage of Robert, Earl of Essex, and Lady Francis Howard, was celebrated in the year 1606. The former was not fourteen, and the latter was thirteen years of age. The union was an unhappy one. The "Diary and Correspondence of John Evelyn, F.R.S.," contains references to early marriages. He wrote, under date of August 1, 1672: "I was at the marriage of Lord Arlington's only daughter (a sweet child if ever there was any) to the Duke of Grafton the king's natural son by the Duchess of Cleveland; the Archbishop of Canterbury officiating, the king and all the grandees being present." The little girl at this time was only five years of age. Evelyn concludes his entry by saying, " I had a favour given to me by my lady ; but took no great joy at the thing for many reasons." Seven years later, the children were re-married, and Evelyn, in his "Diary," on November 6th, 1679, states that he attended the re-marriage of the Duchess Grafton to the Duke, she being now twelve years old. The ceremony was performed by the Bishop of Rochester. The king was at the wedding. "A sudden and unexpected thing," writes Evelyn, "when every-body believed the first marriage would have come to nothing ; but the measure being determined, I was privately invited by my lady, her mother, to be present. I confess I could give her little joy, and so I plainly told her, but she said the king would have it so, and there was no going back." The diarist speaks warmly of the charms and virtues of the young bride ; and he deplores that she was sacrificed to a boy that had been rudely bred.

As might be expected, the facile pen of Samuel

Pepys, the most genial of gossipers, furnishes a few facts on this subject. His notes occur in a letter, dated September 20, 1695, addressed to Mrs. Steward. It appears from his epistle that two wealthy citizens had recently died and left their estates, one to a Blue-coat boy and the other to a Blue-coat girl, in Christ's Hospital. The circumstance led some of the magistrates to bring about a match with the youthful pair. The wedding was a public one, and was quite an event in London life. Pepys says, the boy, "in his habit of blue satin, led by two of the girls, and she in blue, with an apron green, and petticoat yellow, all of sarsnet, led by two of the boys of the house through Cheapside to Guildhall Chapel, where they were married by the Dean of St. Paul's." The Lord Mayor gave away the bride.

The marriage of Charles, second Duke of Richmond, and Lady Sarah Cadogan, daughter of the first Earl of Cadogan, forms an extremely romantic story. It is said that it was brought about to cancel a gambling debt between their parents. The youthful bridegroom was a student at college, and the bride a girl of thirteen, still in the nursery. The young Lord of March pro-tested against the match, "saying surely you are not going to marry me to that dowdy." His protestations were in vain, for the marriage service was gone through, and the twain were made one. They parted after the ceremony, and the young husband spent three years in foreign travel, doubtless thinking little about his wife. At all events on his return he did not go direct to her, but visited the sights in town. On his first attendance at the theatre, a most beautiful lady attracted his attention. He inquired her name, and to his surprise he was told that she was Lady March. The young lord hastened to claim his wife, and they spent together a happy life.

In the reign of William III., George Downing, at the age of fifteen, married a Mary Forester, a girl of thirteen. As soon as the marriage service had been concluded, the pair parted company, the boy going abroad to finish his education, and the girl returning home to resume her studies. After spending some three or four years on the Continent, the husband returned to England, and was entreated to live with his wife. He declined to even see her, having a great aversion to her. The husband's conduct caused his wife to entertain feelings of hatred of him, and both would have been glad to have been freed from a marriage contracted before either were master of their own actions, but they sued in vain for a divorce.

The editor of the "Annual Register," under date of June 8th, 1721, chronicles the marriage of Charles Powel, of Carmarthen, aged about eleven years, to a daughter of Sir Thomas Powel, aged about fourteen. Four years later, Lady Mary Wortley Montagu, in one of her lively letters, refers to the marriage, in 1725, of the Duke of Bedford, at the age of sixteen years.

The General Assembly of Scotland, in 1600, ruled that no minister should unite in matrimony any male under fourteen and any female under twelve years of age. The regulation was not always obeyed. In 1659, for example, Mary, Countess of Buccleuch, in her eleventh year, was married to Walter Scott, of Highchester, and his age was fourteen. As late as the 1st June, 1859, was married, at 15, St. James' Square, Edinburgh, a girl in her eleventh year. The official inspector, when he saw the return, suspected an error, but, on investigation, found it was correct.

Young men and maidens may congratulate themselves on living in these later times, when they may not be united in wedlock before they are old enough to think and act for themselves.

P

## The Passing Bell.

HE passing bell, or soul bell, rang whilst persons were *passing* from this life to that beyond, and it was rung that all who heard it might address prayers to heaven and the saints for the *soul* then being separated from the mortal body. One of the earliest accounts of the use of bells in England is connected with this bell. Bede, in speaking of the death of the Abbess of St. Hilda, says that a sister in a distant monastery thought that she heard in her sleep the well-known sound of the passing bell. She no sooner heard it than she called all the sisters from their rest into the church, where they prayed and sang a *requiem*. To show how persistently the custom was maintained, we may quote from the "Advertisements for due Order," passed in the seventh year of the reign of Queen Elizabeth: " Item, that when anye Christian body is in passing, that the bell be tolled, and that the curate be speciallie called for to comforte the sicke person ; and, after the time of his passinge, to ringe no more, but one shorte peale, and one before the buriall, and another shorte peale after the buriall." In ancient days, the bell rang at the hour of passing, whether it happened to be night or day. In the church-wardens' accounts for the parish of Wolchurch, 1526, appears the following regulation :

"Item. The clerke to have for
tollynge of the passynge belle for
manne, womanne, or childes, if it
be in the day ...................... iiijd.

Item. If it be in the night, for the
same ............................... viijd."

Shakespeare's universal observation led him to make use of the melancholy meaning of the death bell. He says, in the second part of *King Henry IV.*:

> "And his tongue
> Sounds ever after as a sullen bell
> Remembered knolling a departing friend."

The passing bell has a place in the story of the death, in the Tower of London, of Lady Catherine Grey, sister to the unfortunate Lady Jane. The constable of the Tower, Sir Owen Hopton, seeing that the end was approaching, said to Mr. Bokeham : "Were it not best to send to the church, that the bell may be rung ?" and Lady Catherine herself, hearing the remark, said to him : "Good Sir Owen, be it so," and died almost at once, closing her eyes with her own hands. This was in 1567.

The tolling of the passing bell, as such, continued until the time of Charles II., and it was one of the subjects of inquiry in all articles of visitation.

The form of inquiry in the Archdeaconry of Yorke by the churchwardens and sworne-men, in 163–, was : "Whether doth your clark or sexton, when any one is passing out of this life, neglect to toll a bell, having notice thereof, or, the party being dead, doth he suffer any more ringing than one short peale, and before his burial one, and after the same another ?" Inquiry was also to be made : "Whether, at the death of any, there be any superstitious ringing ?" There is a widespread saying :

"When the bell begins to toll,
Lord have mercy on the soul."

Gascoigne, in his "Workes," 1587, mentions

the passing bell in the prefatory lines to a sonnet,
he says :

> " Alas, loe now I heare the passing bell,
> Which care  appoynteth carefully to knowle,
> And in my brest I feele my heart now swell
> To breake the stringes which joynd it to my soule."

Another instance of the poetic use is to be
found in the *Rape of Lucrece*, by Heywood
(1630), where Valerius exclaims : " Nay, if he
be dying, as I could wish he were, I'le ring out
his funerall peale, and this it is :

> Come list and harke, the bell doth towle,
> For some but now departing soule.
> And was not that some ominous fowle,
> The batt, the night-crow, or skreech-owle,
> To these I heare the wild woolfe howle,
> In this black night that seems to skowle.
> All these my black booke shall in-rowle ;
> For hark, still, still, the bell doth towle
> For some but now departing sowle."

Just a little earlier, Copley, in his " Wits, Fits,
and Fancies " (1614), bears evidence to the ringing of the bell while persons were yet alive.  A
gentleman who lay upon a severe sick bed, heard
a passing bell ring out, and thereupon asked his
physician : " Tell me, maister Doctor, is yonder
musicke for my dancing ? "  Continuing the
subject, he gives an anecdote concerning " The

ringing out at the burial." It is as follows: A rich miser and a beggar were buried in the same churchyard at the same time, "and the belles rung out amaine" for the rich man. The son of the former, fearing the tolling might be thought to be for the beggar instead of his father, hired a trumpeter to stand "all the ringing-while" in the belfry and proclaim between every peal, "Sirres, this next peale is not for R., but for Maister N.," his father. In the superstitions which gathered round the bells of Christianity, the passing bell was considered to ward off the influence of evil spirits from the departing soul. Grose says: "The passing bell was anciently rung for two purposes: one to bespeak the prayers of all good Christians for a soul just departing; the other to drive away the evil spirits who stood at the bed's foot and about the house, ready to seize their prey, or at least to molest and terrify the soul in its passage; but, by the ringing of the bell (for Durandus informs us evil spirits are much afraid of bells), they were kept aloof; and the soul, like a hunted hare, gained the start, or had what is by sportsmen called law. Hence, perhaps, exclusive of the additional labour, was occasioned the high price demanded for tolling the greatest

bell of the church, for, that being louder, the evil
spirits must go farther off to be clear of its sound,
by which the poor soul got so much more the
start of them ; besides, being heard farther off, it
would likewise procure the dying man a greater
number of prayers." This dislike of spirits to bells
is mentioned in the "Golden Legend," by Wynkyn
de Worde.

Douce takes the driving away of the
spirits to be the main object in ringing the
passing bell, and draws attention to the woodcuts
in the Horæ, which contain the " Service of
Dead," where several devils are represented as
waiting in the chamber of the dying man, while
the priest is administering extreme unction. Of
course, the interpretation that the spirits are
waiting to take possession of the soul so soon as
disembodied is not necessarily the intentional
meaning. Douce concludes his remarks by an
observation which has escaped the notice of most of
those who have dealt with the subject. He says :
" It is to be hoped that this ridiculous custom will
never be revived, which has been most probably
the cause of sending many a good soul to the
other world before its time ; nor can the practice
of tolling bells for the dead be defended upon any

principle of common sense, prayers for the dead
being contrary to the articles of our religion."
When the English first began to see the apparent
inconsistency of the practice of tolling with their
declared religion, the subject gave rise to much
controversy. The custom had many apologists.
Bishop Hall says : " We call them soul bells, for
that they signify the departure of the soul, not for
that they help the passage of the soul." Wheatly
says : " Our Church, in imitation of the saints in
former ages, calls on the minister and others who
are at hand to assist their brother in his last
extremity." Dr. Zouch (1796) says : " The soul
bell was tolled before the departure of a person
out of life, as a signal for good men to offer up
their prayers for the dying. Hence the abuse
commenced of praying for the dead." He cites
Douce's versified letter to Sir Henry Wotton :

"And thicken on you now, as prayers ascend
To heaven on troops at a good man's passing bell."

Fuller, long before this, in 1647, expresses
some little indignation at hearing a bell toll after
the person had died, as he was thereby cheated
into prayer. He observes : " What is this but
giving a false alarm to men's devotions, to make
them ready to arm with their prayers for the

assistance of such who have already fought the good fight." Dekker, in an evident reference to the passing bell, calls it "the great capon-bell."

From the number of strokes being formerly regulated according to circumstances, the hearers might determine the sex and social condition of the dying or dead person. Thus the bell was tolled twice for a woman and thrice for a man. If for a clergyman, as many times as he had orders, and, at the conclusion, a peal on all the bells to distinguish the quality of the person for whom the people are to put up their prayers. In the North of England, are yet rung nine knells for a man, six for a woman, and three for a child.

## Concerning Coffins.

THE use of the coffin may be traced back to a remote period. The remains of Joseph were conveyed in a coffin from Egypt to Canaan. The Christians adopted their use from the heathen.

Coffins have been made of various kinds of material. Cedar was used for the Athenian heroes on account of its aromatic and incorruptible qualities. It is said that Alexander was buried in one made of gold. Marble and stone were largely used by the Romans, but many lead coffins have been found in the Roman cemeteries at Colchester, York, London, and other places. Coffins of baked clay and cists formed of tiles have been found at York and at Adlborough. Glass coffins have been used in England. Wooden coffins are, in this country, of great antiquity. It is recorded that King Arthur was buried, in 542, in the entire trunk of a tree, hollowed. Some of the earlier coffins made of wood are extremely rude in shape. Abbot Warin, of St. Alban's, 1183-95, gave directions for the monks to be buried in stone coffins. They had previously been buried without coffins, under the green turf. According to an ancient legend, St. Cuthbert's remains sailed down the Tweed in a stone coffin.

Generally speaking, the modes of burying the dead in the Middle Ages were without coffins. The corpses were usually enveloped in linen, but members of religious houses were usually buried in the habit of their order.

Coffins, in their universal use in this country, comparatively speaking, belong to modern times. Thomas Hearne, the antiquary, writing in 1742, says that sixty years before that period it was a common custom to bury the dead without coffins. People of rank, however, were usually buried in coffins, unless they left directions to the contrary.

Sir Walter Scott has made us familiar with the fact that it was customary for

"The lordly line of high Saint Clair"

to deposit their dead in a vault at Roslin Chapel, attired in the armour they had used in life.

In Ireland, there was a curious custom of burying the dead without coffins. "Until about the year 1818," says a correspondent of *Notes and Queries*, Second Series, vol. i., p. 455, "certain families, named Tracey, Doyle, and Daly, of the townland of Craan, near Enniscorthy, in the barony of Scarawalsh, in the county of Wexford, were in the habit of burying their dead uncoffined, in the graveyard attached to the Augustinian Abbey of Saint John. The bodies were brought to the place of sepulture in open coffins, with their faces uncovered. The graves were made six or more feet deep, and lined with bright green turf from the banks of the river Slaney. In these green chambers, were strewn moss, dry grass, and flowers, and a pillow of the same supported the head of the corpse when it was laid in its last earthly bed."

In a "Table of Dutyes" of Shoreditch Church, 1664, are references to the amounts to be paid if coffins are not used at funerals. It is stated, "for a burial in ye new churchyard, without a coffin, eight pence; for a burial in ye olde churchyard, without a coffin, seaven pence; and for the grave-making and attendance of ye Vicar and Clarke on ye enterment of a corps uncoffined, the churchwardens to pay the ordinary duteys, and no more, of this table."

The poor were usually buried in parish coffins, or rather taken from their humble homes to the grave in a coffin, and at the grave removed from it and merely interred in their shrouds. At Easingwold Church, in East Yorkshire, an interesting example of the parish coffin is still preserved. It is strongly and roughly made of oak. We give an illustration of this old-time

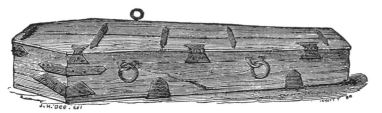

PARISH COFFIN, EASINGWOLD CHURCH.

relic from a carefully-made drawing by Mr. J. H. Doe. In Smith's "Old Yorkshire," vol. v., pp. 106-110, will be found an informing article on the Easingwold and other parish coffins, by the late Llewellynn Jewitt, F.S.A., who collected much out-of-the-way information on this subject. From the Rev. Canon Hayman, he received the following important communication: "The old historical town of Youghal, in the county of Cork," wrote Canon Hayman, "has many features of

interest for the antiquary, chiefest among which
is the venerable Collegiate Church of St. Mary.
The cemetery attached to this noble edifice is the
*Pere la Chase* of Ireland.    The ground naturally
forms a succession of terraces, here swelling into
little knolls, there sinking into gentle declivities.
A poet said of the Protestant burial ground of
Rome : ' It might make one in love with death to
think that one should be buried in so sweet a
place,' and the saying may be repeated of the
Youghal churchyard.    Death is here divested of
its horror, and wears the softened aspect of still-
ness and unbroken repose.    On its northern and
western sides, the cemetery is overhung by the
old walls of the town, which are yet in good
preservation.    In a portion of those defences,
nearly opposite to the western gable of the church,
is a recessed [coffin-shaped] aperture, of which
the accompanying is an engraving.   Here, as the
old folk tell us, was kept the public coffin for the
poor of Youghal.    Whenever needed, it was sent
to the house of the dead ; and, so soon as it had
discharged its office, it was replaced here.    The
walls, as may be perceived, are of three thick-
nesses.    The newest piece, in front, is of
hammered, well-squared masonry.    More ancient

is the furthest drawn, where the materials are less in size, and are less carefully finished ; but, lying between these twain, is a fragment of a very old wall, built of exceeding small stones, and evidently preserved from demolition because of its characteristic feature—the Parish Coffin Recess." It will be observed, from the illustration we give,

RECESS FOR PARISH COFFIN, YOUGHAL CHURCHYARD.

that the recess was coffin-shaped, so that when the parish coffin was not in use it might be placed upright in the place specially prepared for it.

Respecting the parish coffin of Stockton-on-Tees, there is a note in the history of the town, by the Rev. John Brewer, and published in 1796.

It is stated : " Soon after the Rev. Geo. Walker, vicar [1715], came to reside at Stockton-on-Tees, he was called upon to inter a poor person. When they came to the grave, the attendants were preparing to take the body out of the shell or coffin which contained it. He enquired what they were doing, and was informed that the same coffin was used for the funerals of the poor, and that this was intended to serve again. He insisted on its being put into the ground with the body ; and, from this time, took care to prevent a repetition of such an act of indecency."

During the visit of the members of the Yorkshire Architectural Society to Howden, on August 25th, 1885, an old oak parish coffin was inspected by them. It was much dilapidated, but on it could be traced the date, 1664.

We have found in old churchwardens' accounts several entries relating to parish or church coffins. In the Vestry Book of St. Oswald, Durham, are the following items :

" 1614-15. Pd. for mendinge the bell
        wheele, and for makinge the
        coffins for to bringe the dead
        corpes to the church in............ ijs.
    Pd. for bordes for same ............... xxd.

" Pd. for bread and drinke for workmen

    att that tyme ...................... iiijd."

The same parish records for 1666-7 contain an entry as follows :

" For a church coffin .................... 14s."

Parish coffins must have been very distasteful to the poor, for the humbler classes of England dearly love a display at a funeral. An epitaph in St. Michael's churchyard, Macclesfield, illustrates the weakness in this direction in our character. It reads as follows :

" MARY BROOMFIELD,

dyd 19 Novr., 1755, aged 80.

The chief concern of her life for the last 20 years was to order and provide for her funeral. Her greatest pleasure was to think and talk about it. She lived many years on a pension of 9d. a week, and yet saved £5, which, at her own request, was laid out on her funeral."

In the reign of George III., wars prevailed to an alarming extent, and extraordinary taxes were levied to obtain money to maintain the army and navy. Among the proposals made to raise further revenue was a tax on coffins, which gave rise to some keen epigrams. Here are a couple of examples. The first is by Mr. Evans, M.P., and dated Derby, July 6, 1791 :

Q

> " Taxed when we're born and when we die,
>   Must coffins now a tax supply ?
>   In vain on earth we respite crave,
>   Or seek a shelter in the grave ! "

Mr. Evans adverts to the old tax by which persons, not being in the receipt of alms, had to pay two shillings on the birth of a child. The nobility and gentry were taxed at a much higher rate, for example, a duke, for his eldest son, had to pay £30. Another epigrammatist addressed the king as follows :

> " Taxed to the bone, thy loving subjects see !
>   But still supposed, when dead from taxes free ;
>   Now to complete, Great George, thy glorious reign,
>   Excis'd to death, we're then excis'd again."

## The Curfew Bell.

FEW points of national history have given rise to so much discussion as the facts and inferences connected with what is known as the curfew law. The testimony of the various writers on ancient jurisprudence differs widely as to the period at which the law originated, and yet more widely as to the object and intention of those who imposed it upon the people of England. We will first briefly outline the regulation or custom as we find it under the Normans. At eight in the evening, a bell was rung, the sound of which was the signal for everyone to put out, or rather cover, their fires, extinguish all lights, and go to bed. This was the curfew law, which it has been the custom to regard as a repressive measure adopted by the tyrant Conqueror to prevent seditious meetings of the turbulent Saxons. We "find the name of curfew law employed as a bye-word denoting the most odious tyranny, and historians, poets, and lawyers, speaking of it as the acme of despotism, levelled alone at the vanquished English." We will endeavour to show that, on the contrary, the law was in existence and force before the Normans trod the conquered fields of Angle-land, and that its intention was to cherish the good of the country by preventing the rise of conflagrations.

Throughout the north of Europe, in monasteries and towns, a bell for covering of fires was in common use ; a regulation which reason cannot but approve, for most dwellings, even those of the higher classes, were built, for the greater part, of timber, the Saxon term for building being an expression meaning to "make of wood." We read that London and other towns were frequently subject to fires. In England, the curfew law is said to have been made an established institution by King Alfred. When that monarch restored the University which had been founded at Oxford by St. Frideswide, he ordained, among other thoughtful regulations, that a bell should be rung every night at eight, when all the inhabitants of Oxford should cover up their fires and go to bed.

The intention was not that the fires should be put out, but merely deadened. As Mr. Lomax observes, " The old fires were made in the centre of a large hearth, and the accumulated ashes were swept to the back and sides. At the curfew, the large logs were removed, and the cold ashes raked over the fire so as to cover it. A fire so covered will often keep smouldering for days, and can be re-lighted by adding fuel and admitting air, a most important consideration in the days of tinder-boxes. The same custom is still pursued in the backwoods of America, in the Australian bush, and in our own 'black country,' where the great coal fires are 'raked' in the old fashion nightly."

The word *curfew* is derived from the old French *carre-feu* or *cerre-feu*, which afterwards became *couvre-feu*, and lastly *curfew*. Each of these terms, meaning to cover fire, indicates the intention ; and there was a utensil known as the *couvre-feu*, a kind of metal cover, somewhat resembling a shield in form, the use of which was to be thrust over the fire when the bell rang. This probably would only be found in the houses of the wealthy.

King Alfred the Great passed away, and all

the line of Saxon and Danish monarchs after him; yet probably the curfew, under one or another of its ancient names, was kept up as a national observance in each of their reigns, with more or less laxity. At last the Conqueror came, and after that sanguinary struggle, which had to roughly pave the way for England's advancement,

COUVRE-FEU.

he set himself the task of governing the people he had overcome. Whether he found the law of the curfew still feebly kept up, or whether it had died out we cannot tell, but we know that two years after the battle of Hastings—in 1068— he ordered fires to be covered at the ringing of an eight o'clock bell, and the people to retire to rest. He had probably been accustomed to a

similar regulation in Normandy ; and it is evident
the enactment, however more severely enforced
than the Saxons had previously experienced,
could not have been purposed as a suspicious and
contemptuous safeguard against them, for the
haughty robbers called nobles were as subject to
the curfew as the meanest swineherds they owned.
There seems to have been, from an indefinitely
early period, a religious service at eight in the
evening. When William, after the injuries
received by the plunging of his horse as it trod
upon hot ashes, lay dying, the vesper bell of a
neighbouring church aroused him from the stupor
which had gathered round his sinking mind. He
asked if he were in England, and if that were the
curfew ringing, and on being told he was in "his
own Normandy," and the bell was for evening
prayer, he "charged them bid the monks pray
for his soul, and remained awhile dull and heavy."
Polydore-Vergil tells us that William, to convert
the native ferocity of the people to indolence,
ordained that the head of each family should
retire to rest at eight in the evening, "having
raked the ashes over the fire ; and for this purpose
a sign should be made through every village,
which is even now preserved, and called in the

Norman, *cover-feu.*"    Mr. Hutchinson, in his
" History of Durham," speaks of the curfew with
great bitterness : he says that William "under
severe penalties, prohibited the use of fire or
candles when the curfew bell should ring, to
prevent associations and conspiracies.   This bell
was heard by the English as the knell of their
departed liberty, and a repeated testimony of
slavery."

We learn from Du Cange, that the ringing of
the *couvre-feu, ignitegium,* or *peritegium* bell, as it
was called in mediæval low Latin, prevailed
generally in Europe during the Middle Ages as a
precaution against fire ; and this fact is alone
sufficient to justify William in reviving and
extending the law in this country.

Voltaire, in his " Universal History," ridicules
the notion of the curfew being a badge of
degradation ; he observes that " The law, far
from being tyrannical, was only an ancient police,
established in almost all the towns of the north,
and which had been long preserved in the
convents."   And he adds this reason for it : "That
the houses were all built of wood, and the fear of
fire was one of the most important objects of
general police."    Throughout the reigns of

William I., and his son, William II., the curfew
law was rigidly enforced, and, however good its
intentions were, the rigour of its administration
rendered it increasingly obnoxious. The politic
Henry I., in 1103, wisely repealed the
enactment, modifying the law, which, however,
though not compulsory, " settled into a cherished
custom." Though perhaps no longer as Thomson
describes :

> " The shiv'ring wretches at the curfew sound
>     Dejected sunk into their sordid beds,
>   And, through the mournful gloom of ancient times
>     Mus'd sad, or dreamt of better."

Yet the weary yeomen would doubtless for a long
time welcome the hour that heralded rest.
Certainly the name lingered as a dividing period
of the day.

Blackstone says (vol. iv., p. 420) that Henry
"abolished the curfew, for though it is mentioned
in our laws a full century afterwards, yet it is
rather spoken of as a known time of night (so
denominated from that abrogated usage) than as
a still subsisting custom."

Chaucer speaks of it as a time of day :

> " The dede sleep, for every besinesse,
>   Fell on this carpenter, right as I gesse,
>   About curfew time, or litel more."

In the *Antiquarian Repertory*, vol. i., p. 4, it is stated upon the authority of Monsieur Pasquier, that the ringing of the curfew bell was a custom long established in particular towns in France, and originated, as he supposes, in times of tumult and sedition.   But the earliest instance he gives is no farther back than the year 1331, when the city of Laon, which had forfeited its privileges, was reinstated therein by Philip de Valois, who directed that for the future a curfew bell should be rung in a certain tower in that city, at the close of the day.   Pasquier adds, that under the reigns of Charles VI. and VII., it came much into use.

We will now glance over the records of the curfew, as found in deeds, enactments, poetry, and tradition, preserving, as nearly as convenient, a sequence of date.

In the second mayoralty of Sir Henry Colet, knight (father of Dean Colet), A.D. 1495, and under his direction, this solemn charge was given to the quest of wardmote in every ward, as it stands printed in the *Custumary of London:* "Also yf there be anye paryshe clerke that ryngeth curfewe after the curfewe be ronge at Bowe Chyrche, or Saint Brydes Chyrche, or Saint Gyles without Cripelgat, all suche to be presented." Stow may be regarded as corroborating the statement of curfew usage at the two latter churches.

In Stripe's edition of Stow, 1721 (vol. i., b. 3, p. 542), speaking of St. Mary-le-Bow, it is stated that "The parish clerk's office, belonging to this church, was to ring the curfew bell ; as it was to be rung at three other churches in London, at a pretty distance from each other. That, so this notice, all the curfew bells in other parishes might be rung in due season, viz., Barking Church, S. Bride's, and S. Giles's without Cripplegate."

In the articles agreed upon and settled in 22 Henry VIII. (1531), for the guidance of the sexton of Faversham, we read : " Imprimis, the sexton, or his sufficient deputy, shall lye in the church steeple ; and, at eight o'clock every night, shall ring the curfewe by the space of a quarter of an hour, with such bell as of old time hath been accustomed."

In the Middle Ages, so much regard was paid to ringing the *couvre-feu*, that land was occasionally left to pay for it. This feeling appears to have been not altogether extinct, even so late as the close of the sixteenth century, for

in Bishop Hall's "Fourth Satire" occurs the
following :

> "Who ever gives a paire of velvet shooes
> To th' Holy Rood, or liberally allowes
> But a new rope to ring the *couvre-feu* bell,
> But he desires that his great deed may dwell,
> Or graven in the chancel-window glasse,
> Or in his lasting tombe of plated brasse."

In the churchwardens' and chamberlains'
accounts of Kingston-on-Thames, occurs the
following item :

> "1651.   For ringing the curfew bell
>      for one year ........................ £1   10."

According to the Hon. Daines Barrington,
curfew is written *curphour* "in an old Scottish
poem, published in 1770, with many others, from
the MSS. of George Bannatyne, who collected
them in the year 1568." It is observed in the
notes which accompany these poems, that, by
"Act 144, Parliament 13, James I., this bell was
to be rung in boroughs at nine in the evening,
and that the hour was afterwards changed to ten,
at the solicitation of the wife of James VI.'s
favourite, James Stewart. This lends some
countenance to what might otherwise seem
erroneous in the works of the poets and
dramatists. Thus, in the old play of the

*Merry Devil of Edmonton* (1631), the sexton exclaims :

"Well, 'tis nine a clocke, 'tis time to ring curfew."

We fear, however, that Shakespeare cannot be held free from mistake and uncertainty in his fixing of the curfew hour. Thus, in *Measure for Measure*, the Duke says :

"The best and wholesom'st spirits of the night
Invellop you, good Provost! Who call'd here o' late?
*Provost :* None since the curfew rang."

In *The Tempest*, Prospero says :

"You whose pastime
Is to make midnight mushrooms, that rejoice
To hear the solemn curfew."

Again, in *Romeo and Juliet,* he seems to advance the time still further. Lord Capulet is made to say :

"Come stir, stir, stir, the second cock hath crowed,
The curphew bell hath rung, 'tis three o'clock."

In *King Lear,* we also find the curfew considered a midnight bell : "This is the foul fiend, Flibbertigibbett : he begins at curfew, and walks to the first cock."

Instances of land being given for the ringing of the bell are at Mapouder, Dorset, where land was given "to find a man to ring the morning and curfew bell throughout the year," and at Ibberton, in the same county, one acre of land was given for the ringing of the eight o'clock bell, and £4 for ringing the morning bell.

Macaulay, in 1791, says : "The custom of ringing curfew, which is still kept up at Claybrook, has probably obtained without intermission since the days of the Norman conqueror." In winter, and in flat and dangerous localities, the ringing of the bell in the evening has often been the means of safely guiding and sometimes saving the lives of travellers ; and there are instances on record of persons so saved leaving a sum of money for ringing this bell. Such is the story told of a bride who, from an English village, stole out to hide, like another Ginevra, from her friends on the wedding day. The place was near a wide moor, and the girl hid awhile among the furze. When she sought to return, to laugh merrily at the anxious groom and guests, she, alas ! took a wrong path, and presently found herself lost on the waste. The shades of night and the shrouding snow fell fast, and the bride had well nigh given herself up to despair, when, hark ! the curfew bell ! Yes, it is the well-known curfew bell solemnly, and O, how sweetly, pealing from the grey old tower, that overshadowed her home. After being guided to that home by the blessed sound, she presented a chime of bells to the church, and, upon her death, years after, it was found she had bequeathed money to keep up the ringing of the curfew bell for ever.

We may here state that we are indebted for some of the information given in this paper to Mr. H. Syer Cuming. He has also kindly favoured us with facts and suggestions for other chapters included in this volume.

The curfew bell may now be said to be one of the things of the past. True, here and there a bell may ring in the evening from the powerful force of old custom, yet all the associations of the custom itself are lost; the bell summons us from home, not commands to retire to sleep; the *couvre-feu* is a rare object of interest in our museums; and now only in the volumes of the poets shall we find that

" The curfew tolls the knell of parting day."

## Curious Symbols of the Saints.

SOME curious symbols of the saints were carved on ancient clog-almanacks which were in use before the introduction of printing. Even as late as the year 1686, when Dr. Robert Plot compiled his "Natural History of Staffordshire," he tells us that the clog-almanack was "in use among the meaner sort of people." It was largely employed in the northern counties, but Plot failed to trace it further south than the county of Stafford. In Denmark, it was in use in bygone times, and it is supposed to have been introduced into this country by the Danish invaders.

The almanack was usually a square stick made of box or other hard wood, about eight inches in length, and often having a ring at the top for suspending it in a room. It occasionally formed part of a walking stick.

The days of the year are represented by notches running along the angles of the square stick, and in each angle three months are indicated. It will be seen from the picture which forms the frontispiece to this work, that Sunday is marked with a somewhat broader notch than the other days. Its chief interest, however, is on account of representing emblems of the saints, and a few of the more important may be mentioned. On January 13th, is the feast of St. Hilary, and there is a cross or badge of a bishop. An axe, on January 25th, indicates St. Paul's Day. It was with that implement that St. Paul suffered martyrdom. On St. Valentine's Day, is a true lover's knot. For the Patron Saint of Wales, St. David, is a harp. It was on that instrument that he praised God. On March 2nd, the notch ends with a bough, and it is the day set apart to the memory of St. Chad. It is a symbol of the hermit's life he led in the woods near Lichfield. A bough also appears on May 1st, the popular day for bringing home May blossom. A harvest rake is figured on June 11th, which is St. Barnabas' Day. It denotes the time of hay harvest. A sword on June 24th, marks St. John the Baptist's Day. He was beheaded with

R

that weapon.   St. Peter's Day falls on June 29th,
and there are two keys shewn in allusion to his
being recognised as the janitor of Heaven.   On St.
Laurence's Day, August 10th, is a gridiron.   He
displayed firmness and constancy under great
suffering.   He was laid on a gridiron and broiled
to death over a fire.   A wheel, on which St.
Catherine suffered death, represents the day set
apart to her memory.   A decussated cross, on
which St. Andrew was crucified, indicates his
day.   His death was rendered more lingering by
tying him with cords to the cross.   He may
fairly be regarded as one of the most popular of
our saints ; some six hundred churches have been
dedicated to his memory.   This saint is always
represented in pictures as an old man with a long
flowing beard.   On October 25th, is St. Crispin's
Day, the Patron Saint of shoemakers, and, most
appropriately, a pair of shoes marks his day.   The
Feast of St. Clement, November 23rd, is indicated
with a pot.   The symbol is an allusion to the old
custom of going about on that night begging
drink to make merry with.   Christmas Day
is marked with a horn, which has reference to the
custom of the Danes wassailing or drinking
healths, "signifying to us, that this is the time

we ought to rejoice and make merry." We must not omit to add that for the Purification, Annunciation, and all other feasts of our Lady, there is always the figure of a heart.

A careful study of the picture of the clog almanack will reveal other curious matters of interest.

## Acrobats on Steeples.

IN bygone times, the public were often entertained by the performances of acrobats on church steeples. We gather, from the brief particulars which have come down to us of the feats enacted, that they were far from elevating, and it is surprising that the acting was allowed to take place on any part of a church.

Rope dancing was provided and appreciated. At the coronation of Edward VI., a rope was stretched from the battlements of St. Paul's to a window at the Dean's gate, and the king was highly entertained by the capering of a sailor of Arragon on it.

A less successful piece of acting was attempted in 1555, when a Dutchman stood on the top of St. Paul's steeple, and waved a streamer. The wind was high, and the lights could not be kept

burning to enable the public to see him. Sixteen
pounds was paid for the perilous performance.

At Salisbury, a similar foolhardy trick was
enacted by a man who hoped to receive a
gratuity from George III. But the king
declined to give anything, saying: "As the
father of my people, it is my duty to reward those
who save life, and not those who risk human life."

At the reception of King Philip, in 1553, we
are told, "a fellow came slipping upon a cord, as
an arrow out of a bow, from Paul's steeple to the
ground, and lighted with his head forward on a
greate sort of feather bed." This kind of feat
remained popular for a long period. William
Hutton, the historian, saw a man giving a similar
entertainment at Derby, in 1732. Hutton's
account of the affair is full of interest, and we
cannot do better than quote a few particulars
from it. "There are characters," wrote Hutton,
"who had rather amuse the world, at the hazard
of their lives, for a slender and precarious pittance,
than follow an honest calling for an easy sub-
sistence. A small figure of a man, seemingly
composed of spirit and gristle, appeared in
October, to entertain the town by sliding down a
rope. One end of this was to be fixed at the top of

All Saints' steeple, and the other at the bottom of
St. Michael's, an horizontal distance of 150 yards,
which formed an inclined plane extremely steep.
A breast-plate of wood, with a groove to fit the
rope, and his own equilibrium were to be his
security, while sliding down upon his belly, with
his arms and legs extended. He could not be
more than six or seven seconds in this airy
journey, in which he fired a pistol and blew a
trumpet. The velocity with which he flew raised
a fire by friction, and a bold stream of smoke
followed him. He performed this wonderful
exploit three successive days, in each of which he
descended twice, and marched up once; the latter
took him more than an hour, in which he exhibited many surprising achievements, as sitting
unconcerned with his arms folded, lying across
the rope upon his back, then his belly, his hams,
blowing the trumpet, swinging round, hanging by
the chin, the hand, the heels, the toe, etc. The
rope being too long for art to tighten, he might
be said to have danced upon the slack. Though
he succeeded at Derby, yet, in exhibiting soon
after at Shrewsbury, he fell, and lost his life."

He was buried in the churchyard of St. Mary
Friars, Shrewsbury, in 1740, and over his remains

was placed a tombstone, bearing the following
epitaph :

> " Let this small monument record the name
> Of CADMAN, and to future times proclaim
> How, by an attempt to fly from this high spire,
> Across the *Sabrine* stream, he did acquire
> His fatal end. 'Twas not for want of skill,
> Or courage to perform the task, he fell ;
> No, no, a faulty cord being drawn too tight
> Hurried his soul on high to take her flight,
> Which bid the body here beneath, good night."

Hogarth immortalised Cadman in one of his
most popular pictures.

To return to Derby, we find that, in 1734, a
second "flyer" visited the town. He was much
older than the first performer, and less in stature.
" His coat," we are told, "was in deshabille : no
waistcoat ; his shirt and his shoes the worse for
wear ; his hat, worth three-pence, exclusive of the
band, which was packthread, bleached white by
the weather ; and a black string supplied the
place of buttons to his waistband. He wisely
considered, if his performances did not exceed the
other's, he might as well stay at home, if he had
one. His rope, therefore, from the same steeple,
extended to the bottom of St. Mary's-gate, more
than twice the former length. He was to draw a
wheel-barrow after him, in which was a boy of

thirteen. After this surprising performance, an ass was to fly down, armed as before, with a breast-plate, and at each foot a lump of lead about half a hundred. The man, the barrow, and its contents arrived safe at the end of their journey. When the vast multitude turned their eyes towards the ass, which had been braying several days at the top of the steeple for food ; but, like many a lofty courtier for a place, brayed in vain ; the slackness of the rope, and the great weight of the animal and his apparatus, made it seem, at setting off, as if he were falling perpendicularly. The appearance was tremendous ! About twenty yards before he reached the gates of the county-hall, the rope broke. From the velocity acquired by the descent, he bore down all before him. A whole multitude was overwhelmed ; nothing was heard but dreadful cries ; nor seen, but confusion. Legs and arms went to destruction. In this dire calamity, the ass, which maimed others, was un-hurt himself, having a pavement of soft bodies to roll over. No lives were lost. As the rope broke near the top, it brought down both chimneys and people at the other end of the street. This dreadful catastrophe put a period to the art of flying. It prevented the operator from making the intended collection; and he sneaked out of Derby as poor as he sneaked in."

The clergy in Derby, in years agone, appear to have enjoyed popular shows. When Topham, the celebrated strong man, visited the town, in 1737, he performed, among other feats, the following: " He took Mr. Chambers, vicar of All Saints', who weighed 27 stones, and raised him with one hand. His head being laid on one chair and his feet on another, four people, 14 stones each, sat upon his body, which he heaved at pleasure. He struck a round bar of iron, one inch diameter, against his naked arm, and, at one stroke, bent it like a bow. Weakness and feeling seemed fled together. Being a Master of music, he entertained the company with Mad Tom. He sung a solo to the organ in St. Werburgh's church, then the only one in Derby; but though he might perform with judgment, yet the voice, more terrible than sweet, scarcely seemed human. Though of a pacific temper, and with the appearance of a gentleman, yet he was liable to the insults of the rude. The hostler at the Virgin's Inn, where he resided, having given him disgust, he took one of the kitchen spits from the mantel-piece, and bent it round his neck like a handkerchief; but as he did not choose to tuck the ends in the hostler's bosom, the cumbrous ornament excited the laugh of the company, till he condescended to untie the iron cravat."

In 1600, Banks, and his famous horse, Morocco, ascended to the top of St. Paul's. The animal was made to override the vane, much to the astonishment of a large gathering of Londoners. It is related in one of the "Jest Books" of the period that a servant came to his master, who was walking about the middle aisle of the church, to ask him to go and witness the wonderful performance. "Away with you, fool!" answered the gentleman, "what need I go so far to see a horse on the top, when I can see so many asses at the bottom?" In France, Banks and his horse attracted much attention. At Orleans, we are told, the fame they had obtained brought Banks under the imputation of a sorcerer, and he narrowly escaped being burnt at the stake. According to Bishop Morton, Banks cleared himself by commanding his horse to "seek out one in the press of the people who had a crucifix on his hat; which done, he bade him kneel down unto it, and not this only, but also to rise up again, and to kiss it. 'And now, gentlemen,' (quoth he), ' I think my horse hath acquitted both me and himself;' and so his adversaries rested satisfied, conceiving (as it might seem) that the devil had no power to come near the cross." It is stated by several writers that Banks and his horse were burned to death at Rome, "as subjects of the Black Power of the World, by the order of the Pope." Other writers assert that he was living in the days of King Charles as a jolly vintner in Cheapside.

The most serious results of permitting acrobats to perform on churches remain to be recorded. It is related by Raine that, in 1237, Prior Melsonby was elected Bishop of Durham, and that his mitre was taken from him for encouraging a rope dancer to perform his feats on a cord stretched between the towers of the cathedral. The poor fellow fell and broke his neck.

THE END

# Index.

Abjuring the realm, 4
Acrobats on steeples, 244-251
Ale at weddings, 199
Alford, plague at, 164
Armour, buried in, 219

Bainbridge horn, 79
Banks and his horse Morocco, 250
Battle Abbey, 38
Bear-baiting on Sunday, 99
Bedford bridge, 51 ; prison, 51 ;
    Bunyan, 51 ; curious regula-
    tions, 51 ; chapel, 51
Bernwood forest, 72
Beverley sanctuary ; 14, plague at,
    160
Biddenden Maids Charity, 148-151
Bible burned, 127
Boar slaying, 74
Boiling oil, ordeal of, 24
Boiling water, ordeal of, 23
"Book of Sports," 103
Bowling on Sunday, 97
Bradford-on-Avon bridge, 53
Bradley, plague at, 166
Brentwood Church, sanctuary in, 9
Braintree, plague at, 167
Broad-stone, East Retford, 164
Bull-baiting announced in church,
    92
Buried alive, 165
Burning to death, 85

Cadman killed, 247
Carlisle horn, 75
Castleton, curious custom at, 180-
    182
Chapels on Bridges, 44-64

Chairs, sanctuary, 15
Charter Horns, 65-79
Cheapside Cross, 138-147
Chingford horn, 78 ; singular
    tenure, 79
Chimney money, 183-185
Clog almanack, 240
Coining by Archbishop of York, 38
Colchester, plague at, 169
Cold water ordeal, 25
Concerning Coffins, 218-226
Corpse, touching a, 28-36
Craven custom, 202
Cuming, H. Syer, 239
Cross, origin of, 120
Curfew Bell, 227-239
Curious Symbols of the Saints, 240-
    243

Danes, Sunday under, 83
Derby St. Mary's bridge, 54 ;
    chapel, 55 ; Jesuits, 55 ; St.
    James bridge, 56 ; plague, 161 ;
    rope performing, 246 ; Topham,
    249
Durham sanctuary, 12-14 ; parish-
    coffins, 224 ; fatal accident to a
    rope-dancer, 251

Easingwold parish coffin, 221
Easter Sepulchre, 111-119
Eleanor, Queen, 138, crosses, 138
Esk, bridge over, 46
Eyam cross, 121 ; plague, 170-173
Executions, 25, 29, 33, 34, 36, 37,
    56, 85

Fight between the Mayor of Hull
    and Archbishop of York, 37-43

Fined for not attending church, 108-110
Football on Sunday, 96
Friars building bridges, 44

Grave, a man making his own, 167

Hanging, 25-37
Hastings, battle of, 86
Henry I. abolishes curfew law, 233
Hoghton Tower, James at, 102
Hot ale at weddings, 199-202
Howdén parish coffin, 224
Hull merchants evading prisage claims, 39 ; Sunday regulations, 89 ; plague at, 95
Hungerford horn, 77 ; curious customs, 78

Indulgences, 45, 122
Ireland, burials without coffins, 221
Iron, red-hot ordeal, 27

King curing an Abbot of indigestion, 174-176
Kissing the Bride, 195-198
Kissing customs, 78, 107
Knox and Sunday, 98

Leicester, plague at, 158-160
Lich-gates, 139-140
Lincoln, Bishop of, claims right of hanging criminals, 37
London Bridge, 47-50 ; chapel on, 48 ; houses on, 48 ; terrible fire, 48 ; heads of traitors on, 49

Macclesfield, curious epitaph, 225
Manchester sanctuary, 6-7
Manx laws, 192
Markets on Sunday, 86-89
Marriage of a Blue-coat boy, 207
Marriages on Sunday, 98
Marrying Children, 203-209
Marrying under the gallows, 191-194
Marrying in a white sheet, 186-190
Masques on Sunday, 95
Mint belonging to Archbishop of York, 38
Murder in Westminster Abbey, 8-9

New England, Sunday in, 107-108
New York, curious marriage custom, 194

Nigel's horn, 72
Norfolk, Sunday trading in, 91
Northampton, fire at, 183 ; hearth money, 184 ; cross, 139, 141

Oak leaves, carrying, 179
Ordeal, origin of, 22
Oxford, play at, 95

Passing Bell, 210-217
Penance of Jane Shore, 125
Penderel's grave, 178
Plagues and Pestilences, 152-173 ; business stopped, 152 ; watch and ward, 153 ; red crosses on doors, 154 ; dogs killed, 154 ; strange remedies, 155 ; Newcastle, 158 ; Leicester, 158 ; Derby, 162; Smoking, 163 ; Broad-stone, East Retford, 164 ; Alford 164 ; burial of dead, 165 ; buried alive, 165 ; Stratford-on-Avon, 165 ; Bradley, 166 ; Braintree, 167 ; Colchester, 169 ; collections, 170 : Eyam, 170
Plays on Sunday, 92-96
Preaching, extravagant, 133
Puritans and Sunday, 101, 104-147
Pusey horn, 70

Reading Abbey, 174
Red-hot iron ordeal, 27
Rhyne Toll, 73
Right of Sanctuary, 1-21
Ringing on May 29th, 183
Romance of Trial, 23-26
Rotherham Bridge, 56 : chapel, 56
Rope dancers, 244-251

St. Paul's Cross, 120-137 ; oaths taken at, 122 ; thrown down by an earthquake, 122 ; indulgences granted for assisting to rebuild it, 122 ; penance at, 124-125 ; sermon in favour of the Duke of Gloucester, 126 ; Bible burned at, 127 ; riot at, 128 ; Queen Elizabeth's love of display, 129; Hooker at Shunamite House, 131 ; rioters at, 131 ; James I. at, 133 ; pulled down, 136
Sales, etc., announced by parish clerks, 92

Salford bridge, 51 ; chapel on, 51 ; prison on, 51
Salisbury, tricks on steeple at, 245 ; Cadman killed, 247
Sanctuary, origin of, 1
Sanctuary, right of, 1-21
Saxons, Sunday under, 82
Sorcery at Dalkeith, 35
Scotchman knocking at York gates, 102
Scotland, Early marriages in, 209
Secrets of the realm, disclosing, 5
Services and customs of Royal Oak Day, 179-185
Shunamite House, 131
Skelton in Westminster sanctuary, 10
Slavery in England, 84
Sports on Sunday, 100
Stafford sanctuary, 11
Stage plays in churches, 92-96
Stockton-on-Tees parish coffin, 223
Stoning to death, 85
Stratford-on-Avon, plague at, 165
Sunday in the Olden Time, 81-110
Survival of ordeal, 36
Swords, wearing, 5

Tax on coffins proposed, 225

Tewkesbury, battle of, 7
Thief, hanging a, 37
Traitors' heads on London bridge, 49
Travelling in the olden time, 79
Trial, romance of, 22-36
Tobacco fines, 108
Touch, ordeal of, 28-36

Ulphus, horn of, 65

Wakefield Bridge, 59; chapel, 59; battle, 60
Walking on Sunday forbidden, 107
Water ordeals, 24-25
Westminster Sanctuary, 10
Wigton, meat at church door, 90
William I. enforces curfew law, 233
Whipping to death, 86
Whitton, marriage custom at, 199
Worcester, Sunday trading at, 90 ; battle of, 178

York gates closed on Sunday, 101
York bridge over Ouse, 50 ; chapel, 50
Youghal parish coffin, 221